"This is a readable and provocative book . . ."
—Larry McMurtry
Author, *Lonesome Dove*

"I had to learn to deal with death in the most brutal fashion, when I lost my young daughter, Alex, to cystic fibrosis, but all of us must approach that ultimate question, and Margo Drummond's book is a superb Guide to the mysteries of the end."
—Frank Deford
Author, Alex, *The Life of a Child*

"The book 'humanizes' dying and will be an important source of information for individuals interested in the topic either from an academic or a personal point of view."
—E. Darracott Vaughan, Jr., M.D.
New York Presbyterian Hospital

"If you seek to spiritually enhance your life, this book is for you. Margo Drummond, an experienced educator, deals courageously with death and dying, a topic that she has been teaching for many years. With great sensitivity she teaches us that acceptance of the inevitable end will add meaning to and enhance our appreciation of life itself."
—Rabbi Ze'ev Harari
Mayim Rabim Congregation
Minneapolis, Minnesota

"Outstanding book - It does not paint any false pictures of choices we face or what someone will go through after losing a loved one."
—Kevin Wheeler, Secretary Treasurer
Arizona State Funeral Directors

"Margo's book is rich with details and insights, but she doesn't hit you over the head and overwhelm you with them. She shares just enough to inform you, the way a good, but knowledgeable, friend would over a cup of coffee at the kitchen table."

—Richard Kenyon
Former Book Editor, Milwaukee Journal

BLESSINGS OF
BEING MORTAL

BLESSINGS OF BEING MORTAL

HOW A MATURE UNDERSTANDING OF DEATH CAN FREE US TO LIVE WISELY AND WELL

Margo Drummond

North Star Publications
Sandwich, Massachusetts

Copyright ©2001 Margo Drummond

ISBN: 1-880823-25-X

Cover Photo: Tamsen E. George
Cover Concept: Veronique Cormier
Cover Design: Salwen Studios, Keene, NH
Typesetting/Layout: CGS Inc., Alymer, PQ, Canada

North Star Publications/Ant Hill Press
P.O. Box 227
East Sandwich, MA 02537
(508) 420-6188
fax (508) 420-6570
www.northstarpublications.com

Printed in the United States of America

Publisher's Cataloging in Publication
Drummond, Margo
    Blessings of being mortal: how a mature understanding of death
        can free us to live wisely and well / Margo Drummond — 1st
        ed.
        p. cm.
    Includes bibliographical references and index.
    ISBN: 1-880823-24-1
    1. Death. 2. Conduct of life   I. Title
BD444.D78 2001   128'.5
                                                   QB101-200292

This book is dedicated to my wise and buoyant husband, Jim, who when asked why he was always so happily laughing and singing, replied: "Because I'm alive."

Table of Contents

Foreword

We who are alive today have at least one thing in common with all people who have ever lived. We had no choice about being born! As a comic strip character in the midst of a bad day put it, "Hey, why didn't someone ask me if I wanted to come into this world?" It's true that no one consulted us. No one asked us if we wanted to live this life.

Most of us have something else in common: we believe we do have some choice about how we will live— about how we will use the 40, 50, 60, 70, 80 or 100 years of time and energy which we call our lifetime. We believe we have some choice about whether our life will be full or flat, bold or bland, impassioned or impassive.

The book you are about to read will time and time again remind you that we all have something else in common: our life on earth will end one day. Understandably, we prefer not to think about that reality, for it reminds us of the painful losses and separations we and others will experience when that time comes. And yet, ironically, it is in facing that final commonality called death that can enable us to live more fully and freely. The denial of the reality of death deceives us into thinking that we have forever to live, and therefore often deprives us of truly living in the here and now. The acceptance of the reality of death and the fact that we don't have forever to live on earth can free us—to make the most of the time we have.

Elisabeth Kübler-Ross is known internationally for her writing and lectures on death and dying. Her insights are based on her conversations with hundreds of dying women, men and children. Once she was being interviewed on a national T.V. program and the host asked her a question she had not been asked before. The host asked,

"Dr. Ross, on the basis of your work with all those dying people, what advice would you give to the living?" She sat silently for what seemed to be a long time, and then she said, "After being with so many dying people, what would I say to the living? Oh, this: 'do it now.'" That short statement summed up her conviction that thinking about death and dying can and should get us to the business of life and living.

That is clearly the conviction of Margo Drummond, the author of this book. I first met her more than twenty years ago when she was working on a Master's Degree at Carthage College and taking a course, then called Death and Dying. I learned she had developed and was often teaching a similar course at the high-school level. I was often impressed by her exceptional insights and was privileged to read her well-researched and well-written scholarly papers.

In the pages that follow she shares more of those insights and a wealth of information. The insights and information are based on her own experiences with death; her wide-ranging research; her extensive travels to other lands with an awareness of other cultures' ideas about death; her knowledge of current and controversial death-related issues; and her teaching of—and learning from—thousands of students. She invites and encourages us to reflect on and take a position on a wide variety of practices and issues related to death, dying and grieving. More than that, time after time she challenges us to think personally about life and death—our own life and death, and the life and death of those near and far. She does so with the passionate conviction and hope that facing our common final experience will give us new reasons to choose to live and to love.

Dudley Riggle
Emeritus Professor of Religion
Carthage College

Acknowledgement

I would like to thank the following individuals, groups and organizations for their contributions to this endeavor. Though some may not be individually recognized, due to the limitations of space, each of your names, nonetheless, belongs on this book. So it is with gratitude to:

My students, whose enthusiasm and encouragement inspired its writing.

My publisher, George Trim, who expressed his belief in the work by allowing it to stand unaltered.

Those who critiqued the manuscript—my sister, Cynthia Dennis; my friend, Susan Warren: and my copy-editor, Richard Kenyon and Janis.

Those who provided professional expertise and aided in research—Kevin Wheeler, Rabbi Ze'ev Harari, Dr. Richard Minton, Tom Terry (Racine County Medical Examiner) and the staff of the Racine Public Library.

Those, who unlike myself, possess the computer skills necessary to put the content into manuscript form—Carol and Rachel Cote, Judy Smith, Chris Paulson, and Wendy Martin.

Those dedicated individuals to whom I listened and from whose caring and compassion came much of the content—rescue squad members, emergency room personnel, health care providers, hospice workers, funeral directors, cemetery employees, grief counselors and therapists, and religious leaders.

Those who affirmed my work through the generosity of their endorsements.

So many whose regular inquiries and thoughtful responses with regard to how things were going made more difference than you will ever know.

And most of all to my husband, Jim, who makes every day a day filled with blessings of being mortal.

"Whither Thou Goest"

Whatsoever thy hand findeth to do, do it with all thy might, for there is no work, nor device, nor knowledge, nor wisdom, in the grave, whither thou goest.

—Ecclesiastes

People often ask me why I spend so much time thinking about death. My answer is that whatever one believes about death is really a statement of what one believes about life. The fact that death is the antithesis of life means it is death that gives life perspective. With death as a part of our consciousness, we cease to measure time as limitless. Instead time becomes precious in its finitude. When we accept that we are mortal, and only then, does the joy of simply being alive have an impact on each moment of our being.

As strange as it might seem, death has become for me my best and favorite teacher, not an easy or initially welcome one, but the one that has taught me the most about living. I was barely 16 years old when it seriously occurred to me that there was this thing called DEATH. While our English teacher sat on a window ledge reading aloud to us from Shakespeare one glorious September morning, it somehow came to me that I could die. As I absorbed the words of *Macbeth*, my personal thoughts of death focused on how life could be tragically and irrevocably wasted in pursuit of such folly as money, power and a title. When what really mattered was that all of these people needlessly dying in such pursuit meant that they could never again see late September sunlight ethereally filtering down. What if I died before next September, before I could feel and see the sun in just that way again?

Several weeks later, we were asked by our teacher to write a theme inspired by something we had learned in class. I wrote about the day of my death. When I read the theme aloud to my classmates, as was required, they reacted with surprise at the choice of topic, and not unpredictably. Sixteen-year-olds are immortal in their own minds; they do not die. It is only the old who die.

A year later, President John F. Kennedy was shot to death in Dallas, followed by the assassinations of Dr. Martin Luther King Jr., and John Kennedy's brother, Senator Robert Kennedy. Those killings prompted my college roommate and me to begin discussing our own feelings about death in some detail. During her freshman year of medical school, that college roommate was kidnapped and murdered. She has already been dead for thirty years that I have been alive. I still think of her and reflect on all that I have experienced and seen that she did not.

When I first proposed teaching a class on issues of death and dying the response was not altogether unpredictable. Some of my colleagues dubbed me "D. D.," and posed such questions as, "What are you going to teach them in that class, how to die?" The 16-year-olds, meanwhile, were signing up in such numbers for the class that some had to be turned away for lack of space. Their own sense of invincibility made it, at least outwardly, a nonthreatening adventure based on the premise that the young cannot die. It was that very premise that made them such receptive pupils.

Every 10 weeks a new group of students would assemble, each with a personal agenda. Over and over again I watched them begin their odyssey with a mixture of fear and bravado. At the conclusion of the 10 weeks there was always a change—the fear was gone, or at least greatly diminished, and there was no more need for bravado. What replaced them was an emotional vulnerability exemplified by the final activity of the class. It was called "A Celebration of Life."

For the activity, the students were asked to explain (and bring with them, if possible), whatever gave them the greatest sense of joy in life. As a young man in a film we used for the class had said, in describing the death of his grandfather, "Well I was sixteen, and you're not supposed to cry when you're sixteen." But they did cry as they recalled parents and grandparents, aunts and uncles, brothers and sisters, nieces and nephews, cousins and school chums and even pets, including a lizard concealed in a girl's plastic purse, that had made them feel loved in such special ways.

A remembrance that I shared with the students during our celebration was of a white, saucer-less coffee cup that my mother had given me before she died. She had handed it to me as I was leaving after a 10-day visit with her that each of us assumed would be our last due to the advanced stage of her cancer. How many times had we sat together at her kitchen table sharing deep and intimate secrets over coffee. "Think of me," she said, "when you are having coffee, and use this cup." Once each day I hold that cup against my cheek and think of my mother. As I told the students, that daily gesture represents a link to her more meaningful than any material possession ever could.

Someone walking in on us during one of these celebrations would have to wonder how we could be teary-
eyed over a wrench or a rottweiler, an envelope or an ear-
ring, but that was the magical part. It all came down to
those simple remembrances represented by such gestures
as telling your mom how much you loved her before your
harshest critics, your peers. It was about reaffirming the
lives of those who had died and perhaps left as a reminder
some tangible gift to be treasured. Most of all it was
acknowledging that life should be celebrated each and
every day while it still could be.

Later chance encounters with former students who
had taken the class would almost invariably evoke a comment from them about a personal experience with death.
Often the comment had to do with the perspective they
had gained on the main issue that life presents, human
mortality. It was the most worthwhile and useful part of
their education, many of them concluded.

There was the drug-addicted young man who quietly admitted that nothing in his life had ever made sense
until he sorted through his feelings about issues of dying
and of death. He gave up the use of drugs. There was the
girl whose boyfriend was killed in a drive-by shooting,
who finally began to confront her own fears about death.
During our funeral home visit she sobbed that she could
now visit his grave site for the first time, and then begin to
move on with her own life. And another student who said
that she never could have handled the shock of attending
the visitation and funeral of her employer — where she
witnessed the woman's husband following his wife's casket, their infant daughter in his arms—had she not been
prepared with knowledge and perspective garnered from
this class.

One student told of talking to a parent about death
and learning during the course of the conversation about a

miscarriage that had not been spoken of before. A male student resolved not to waste his life in an alcoholic stupor as he had watched his father doing. And a young woman, inspired by a hospice volunteer who spoke to the class, decided to become a hospice volunteer herself. It took a lot of persuasion to convince the hospice people that a 16-year-old could manage such a thing, but she succeeded not only with them, but with the patients who welcomed her youthful vibrancy and energy. She went on to study medicine.

It was neither an easy, nor always a pleasant process these young people went through in order to gain a perspective on death and dying sufficient to help them restructure their lives. It probably won't be easy or always pleasant for you either. So why proceed? Because there IS this thing called death, which, whether we are 16 or 106, will inevitably fly in our faces. We can, as we did with our childhood slinky toy squeezed into the cylindrical can, push death down and secure the lid on it tightly, but by doing so its ultimate impact will only be greater.

The tension that we create whenever we seek to avoid emotional conflict rather than resolving it simply makes it worse. Death is no different in that regard. The mastery of death—placing it in its proper perspective, where it becomes a tool used to enrich the finite allotment of time called life—is the alternative to ignoring or attempting to escape or expunge its ever-presence from our existence. In choosing the latter, all of those energies that could and should have been applied to living honestly, and thereby happily, are instead channeled into endless feats of delusion.

On many days, as the students were leaving class, I would ask them to remember that any day you are alive is a good one. For them, I trust it will be. They would wish the same for you. All that is required is an understanding

Chapter One

Can Death Teach Us How To Live?

The first step in being happy is realizing you are going to die
—Unknown

What will that day be like, the day you die? Will it be a warm autumn afternoon or a soft spring morning, a bitter January night or a languid summer evening? Will you die at home in your bed, or, as with almost 80% of all Americans, in a hospital or a nursing home? And who or what will be with you when you die—nurses, doctors, life-support systems, tubes and needles—or will you die alone?

What will have preceded your death—a lingering illness, debilitation, pain, disfigurement, lawsuits over your right to die? Will the latest medical technology breathe your last breath, or will you? And what will follow in the moments and hours after you die, an autopsy? Will your body be embalmed, cosmeticized, shown at a viewing? Will organs be removed for science? Will your funeral be a celebration of your life or a cause for the mourning of missed opportunities?

If you are already having trouble imagining all of this, consider yourself normal. Psychologists estimate that we humans can focus on our non-existence for an average of about 10 seconds or less. Even during that time we are imagining a death in which we are still a conscious participant.

Death is such a sobering, depressing topic, so final. Our unconscious refuses to believe in its own death, according to Sigmund Freud. Consequently we behave as if we were immortal. So what's wrong with that, why dwell on our inescapable fate? What's to be gained? The answer is EVERYTHING that constitutes the joy of living. It is only when we allow death to teach us that life is finite, miraculous, a mysterious gift with which we are fleetingly entrusted that we can learn to be happy.

But, you say, thinking about death doesn't make one happy, rather only more anxious about its inevitability. And if we allow ourselves to recognize that every day might be our last, how could we rationally invest in the future? What would be the point?

Certainly it is necessary for our minds to protect us from the overwhelming terror of extinction. But it is also true that the more time and effort and energy we expend on helping those protective mental processes to remain in place, the further we become removed from the reality, and therein, the joy of life. We numb ourselves to life's finitude and its fragility. We deny what Camus referred to as "the benign indifference of the universe" toward our existence or our extinction. We delude ourselves into believing that if one is young and physically strong and socially prominent and politically powerful and wealthy and emotionally involved—and thereby seemingly indispensable and irreplaceable—one cannot die.

We attempt to distance ourselves from death through all of these layers of protection. And then the news of the death of a Princess Diana or a John F. Kennedy, Jr., breaks through and we know that as the comedian W. C. Fields so aptly put it, "None of us, sick or well, can tell when the fellow in the bright nightgown is coming to pay us a visit."

What do we fall back on during those times when our mortal vulnerability is made transparent? We are suddenly forced to ask the question that we should have been seeking an answer to each day of our lives, the question of what is REALLY important. What should I be focusing my energy and attention on? How do I feel about my relationships with other people? How am I managing and spending this daily allotment of time we call life?

When I ask myself that question, about what's really important, I invariably think of my mother who died of ovarian cancer at the age of 64, two months to the day from when it was first diagnosed. I still see her lying on her bed, frail and frightened. She was talking to a family member and her words could have been her own epitaph. "I feel like I wasted it all," she said.

Why she chose to share that most revealing admission was evident. She was issuing a warning not to do what she had done. She, too, had been addicted to alcohol and anti-depressant drugs. She had, in some sense, "wasted it all" on an alcoholic husband whose narcissism had overpowered all her attempts at personal happiness. She had ended up depressed and resentful and eventually broken, not only in spirit but in health. It was too late. She was dying and she knew it. She had squandered her one and only chance to live.

In her book, *Death and the Creative Life*, Lisl M. Goodman asked self-actualized, creative, successful, inventive people—artists and scientists—to examine their feelings about death. Her premise was that people who fit that profile would and should fear death less because of their well-spent lives. Some of the questions she asked them revolved around what they wanted out of life, what they considered to be their highest or ultimate goals, what they considered to be the height of fulfillment, and whether they thought they would ever reach it.

Following those questions were others concerning their personal perspectives on time. The subjects were asked whether they focused primarily on the past, the present or the future. Also she asked if they were aware of the limited amount of time available to them. And finally, were they afraid of death and how often did they think about their own death?[1] The point of Goodman's questions are summarized in the closing paragraphs of her book, in which she wrote:

One of the most devastating consequences of our present unawareness of our limited time span are the regrets—most bitter regrets—of all the things we did or did not do, of all the unspoken words we wanted to utter which must forever remain unsaid, the regrets of thoughts and feelings and of time not shared with one another, the regrets of having let great moments slip by without realizing each one of them alone could have made living and dying worthwhile. . . . But there is no making up once death intervenes. No making up can occur in the last hour, the last month, the last year for a lifetime of missed opportunities.[2]

She concludes with a quote from the poet Ted Rosenthal who died from leukemia at the age of 32. Said he, "I don't think people are afraid of death, what they are afraid of is the incompleteness of their life."[3]

There is a wonderful scene in George Kaufmann's stage play, *You Can't Take It With You*, in which Grandpa engages Mr. Kirby in a philosophical conversation about the value of spending time on things you hate. "Didn't you ever have dreams," Grandpa asks, "something you wanted to do just because it made you happy?" "Of course," responds the workaholic, rich and very unhappy Mr. Kirby, "but what if nobody worked?" "What if everyone just did what made him or her happy? What kind of a world would we have?"

Some years ago, the social critic Michael Kilian wrote an essay in which he, as Kaufmann did in his play, questioned our emphasis on work and acquisition to the exclusion of simple pleasures derived from having time for fun and leisure. How often, he asked, do any of us have an hour, let alone a day, to do just as we please? In our quest for bigger houses, faster cars, chore-saving appliances and buff bodies, we toil at relaxation. Even the rich do. No longer indulging in pleasurable pursuits, they are dealing and dashing about along with the rest of us. What is lost in the process, he concludes, is the realization that time is not money. Time is life.[4]

In an episode of the TV sitcom *Third Rock From The Sun*, the space alien characters try to understand such human attitudes toward money and time. They determine that everyone here on earth sells their time by the hour, like taking a mortgage out on their lives. Why do we assume that life comes with a guarantee of time? And yet, don't we?

My husband and I once met a wealthy toy manufacturer who like ourselves was vacationing on a remote Greek island. As the three of us watched local fishermen patiently repairing their nets, the wealthy man lamented that all of his money could not be traded for even a few hours of a Greek fisherman's life, no matter how willing that fisherman to exchange years of drudgery for a shortened life of financial gain. "I have so much money and so little time," he mused, "they have so much time and so little money. What irony in it all."

Over a thousand years ago the Roman emperor Marcus Aurelius sagely advised that one should approach each task in life, from hour to hour, as if it were to be the last. What if indeed it were your last cup of coffee, the last look at the sky, the last smile from a friend, the last hug from a loved one? Well, do you know that it isn't? And should it be, could you deal with the consequences? What would you most regret then, what would you long for?

Often when I hear someone saying, "Oh, I can't eat that, it's too fattening or not good for me," I think of a woman with terminal cancer who, when asked what she most regretted having not done in life, responded, "If I had known I was going to die I would have eaten more ice cream." When Doris Lund asked her 21-year-old son, Eric, who was near death from leukemia, what she could do for him, he replied, "When you leave here today, don't run for the bus, take your time, walk in the world for me."[5]

Taking time to walk in the world, to eat more ice cream, to feel the sun on your toes, to sit on the porch and talk, to do something just because it makes you happy—that is what death can teach us—to savor the unknown and thereby infinitely more precious quantity of time we are given, understanding that time does not return.

There is a joy that comes with such an understanding. Those who possess that joy have effectively answered the question, why think about death? And their answer is a simple one. Thinking about death forces us to think about life, to accept and cherish the moment as being enough in itself. In our frantic effort to deny and repress and escape and nullify death it is the moment that we miss. And what is the outcome? Not happiness, certainly, just look around you. Where are the truly happy people? Who are they?

It is so basic, really, the moment in which we are living, and so tragically misspent as we dream and drug and wish and work and worry our lives away. And then we die, most of us without ever having understood that life is not too short, it is just that we waste so much of it—on regrets over an irretrievable past and longing for a future that may never come.

Perhaps that is what the Italian actor Marcello Mastroianni was referring to when he characterized human life as, "nearly a total misunderstanding." And yet, as he neared his death at the age of 72, he proclaimed his personal enjoyment of every single day he had lived, (even those during World War II. when he struggled to survive). "I feel," he said, "like I just got here."

Isn't that something that more of us should be able to say, that we are truly deriving pleasure from each day we are alive, that we too feel like we just got here? Wouldn't life and death fall into proper perspective were we able to do so? Wouldn't we have resolved that "nearly total misunderstanding" were we but able to integrate the realities of death into our awareness of what it means to be alive?

Chapter Two

Are We Truly A Death-Denying Culture?

Death is a trick done with mirrors.
                                        —Noel Coward

It's Friday night. The pseudo-sophisticated room is filled with seekers. Parading in the latest fashions from last Saturday's shopping foray, they endure the primal scrutiny that renders their finery moot. Only surreptitious glances garner the desperately desired feedback. Time to alight somewhere, relax oneself with a libation and plunge into mindless banality of small talk, blessedly limited by the too-loud music.

It's Saturday morning. After a workout, back to the mall for more shopping. Maybe this time the effort will be rewarded. Perhaps on Sunday morning the seeker will not wake up alone in his or her bed. Perhaps instead, he or she will escape into the anesthetizing arms of someone, anyone, who can distance the dread, which is death.

Modern man, noted Ernest Becker in his book, *The Denial of Death,* drinks and drugs himself out of awareness, or he spends time shopping, which is the same. English essayist, J. B. Priestley, observed that no culture in the world seems more afraid of even the word death than our own. At dinner parties he would bring up the question of death just to study the stunned reaction. He said people switched off the subject as if they were changing television channels. Arnold Toynbee, in his comments on American attitudes toward death, concluded that our quest for what we feel the Constitution guarantees us—"life, liberty, and the pursuit of happiness" excludes the notion of death as an interloper on the American dream.

Are we truly a death-denying culture? Have we become slaves to the worship of youth as we seek to escape the visible ravages of age that we equate with death—graying hair, wrinkles, sags and bags? Are we wedded to the notion that some technological wonder out there will save us from dying, regardless of how terminal our condition? Have we become a people on a mission not to die? As Octavio Paz noted:

Everything in our consumer society functions as if death did not exist. Nobody takes it into account, it is suppressed everywhere; in political pronouncements, commercial advertising, TV sitcoms and popular customs. Not only has consumerist materialism sought to suppress death in its one-dimensional focus on the present; it now seems possessed by the Promethean desire to "cure" death with technology. This seems to me the ultimate fixation on achieving "paradise now," a vulgar version of hedonism quite unlike the hedonism of Epicurus who lived sensually, but in full knowledge and acceptance of the limits of life.[1]

It is true that our incessant worship of youth and technology makes it more difficult for our psyches to cope with the cognitive dissonance of youth and beauty reduced to rotting flesh. Attempting to remove all outward vestiges of decay and aging may at least fool oneself, if not death. Anything from aerobic exercise a la Jane Fonda or Raquel Welch to increasingly-popular plastic surgery, reportedly practiced by such ageless wonders as Elizabeth Taylor and Cher, attests to our holy war against that inevitable demise.

Cher, who admitted to all but killing herself to keep her youthful body, personifies the fantasy. Featured as one of the "Over 40 and Fabulous," she once was caught disrobing in the back of a limousine whose windows she mistakenly thought were darkened. Commented one riveted voyeur, "Her body is like a 20-year-old's."

Those who attempt to avoid coming face to face with the gut-wrenching realities of death through youth worship may also turn to technology as a form of escape. Like Ponce de Léon's Fountain of Youth, those who wish to avoid death pin their hopes on recent advances in cloning, medical and technological discoveries that may prolong our lives, as well as the ultimate possibility of leaving our mortal bodies behind as we roam the otherworldly reaches of cyberspace. For each possibility there arises a plethora of ethical and social problems not the least of which is how to allocate dwindling resources to a burgeoning and increasingly aged population.

Robert J. Lifton, who has written extensively on the subject of our death-denying culture, believes that the youth of this country dissociate themselves from the realities of death by shopping, rather than having to confront more profound issues related to the meaning of life and the certainty of death. Psychologically it helps to distance death when new clothes and shoes are waiting to be worn in that conceived future, guaranteed by the possession of such objects. Worrying over what kind of jeans or sneakers one is wearing keeps those existential questions of life and death at bay. Society's disenfranchised youth, those who economically cannot participate in the unceasing escape of shopping, participate by taking the sneakers, jackets and jeans from those who can, often discarding what they've taken almost immediately. More and more frequently, violence and death are part of this act.

Our denial of death may be leading to a new type of pornography of death in which violence and death are glorified for their own sake, cautions one psychologist. Could he be right? One wonders how much further an individual can separate his or her feelings about death than to kill without any sense of wrongdoing, as we keep bearing witness to in our society. Neither the objects nor the victims involved are oftentimes even acknowledged as having existed. The objects are dumped, the victims are forgotten, and the taking of life is reduced to this statement by a Washington, D.C. youth, who after a random drive-by shooting of a woman he had never seen before, said simply, "I felt like killing."

What cannot be obliterated by possessions and shopping or violent acts of crime may be obliterated through alcohol, drugs and sex. A recent survey of high school students revealed that over 65% drank more than five times per week. Why does a 15-year-old need to deaden his or her brain cells that often? And even in the face of the AIDS epidemic plaguing this nation, how is it that a middle-class teenager admits to having unprotected sex with 12 to 15 partners between her freshman and sophomore years in high school? The obituary of rapster Eric Wright, known as "Eazy-E," may hold some clues.

"Eazy-E," whose rap group N.W.A. sold millions of records and pioneered the hard-core "gangsta" rap sound, died just ten days after revealing he had AIDS. He was 31. The rapper, whose real name was Eric Wright, was a former drug dealer who claimed to have fathered seven children by six different women. . . . Wright died at Cedars-Sinai Medical Center with his mother and his wife, Tomika by his side. He was hospital-

ized Feb. 24 for what he thought was asthma. Tests showed he had AIDS. He lost his ability to communicate several days ago. Born in the grim Los Angeles suburb of Compton, Wright brought a brutal vision of Los Angeles-area ghetto life to popular art. . . . N.W.A., which stands for Niggaz Wit' Attitude, scored a hit in 1988 with "Straight Outta Compton," which used a thumping beat to tell crude tales of drive-by shootings, drugs, and police harassment. . . . Critics called gangsta rap violent and sexist for its portrayal of police as targets and women as "bitches and whores." Supporters said the songs merely offered the grim reality of the inner city.[2]

Perhaps Eric Wright personified what that psychologist identified as the link between death-denial and the glorification of violent death. Or are the observations of a Midwest funeral director more to the point—when he noted that we aren't so much a death-denying culture as a death-accepting one, to the point where affective feelings related to grief and loss, once associated with death, have been visibly expunged?

Young people in particular, the funeral director stated, don't often show sorrow at funerals anymore. The visitation and funeral activities more closely resemble something akin to "party-time." At the funeral of an infant, he noted, neither parent seemed outwardly aggrieved. They didn't cry but rather smiled and chatted as they gathered their other children around the casket for a family photo.

A century ago, all of these people, "Eazy-E" included, probably would have experienced death in a much different way. Having to stand at the bedside of a dying relative or friend and witnessing him or her die, having to help to wash and dress the corpse, or to help make the coffin or dig the grave, humanized somehow the natural and inevitable outcome of life, which is to die. Such direct and intimate involvement in the process disallows the ability to deny it.

Today's youth may never even see an animal die, let alone a loved one. Someone else is responsible for every aspect of death including keeping the reality of it from us. When a death does occur, to what or to whom can the young turn for answers? Can they turn to adults who are equally unfamiliar and uncomfortable with the process and ritual of dying? Can they turn to those who spend their time and energy denying that death actually happens? Is it any wonder that we are turning out generations who regard death as being no more tangible than their favorite TV character being killed and brought back to life, only to be killed again?

When neither the glorification of youth nor the worship of technology can frighten reality away, we may turn to what Robert Lifton categorizes as attempts to achieve immortality—the biosocial, which is a sense of living on through one's children; the religious, which promises some form of afterlife; the natural, which assumes that we become part of nature when we die or that nature will survive us; the creative, which focuses on what we may write or draw or paint or build or invent for future generations; and transcendence, which would take us beyond the limitations of mortal being.[3]

The desire for biological or biosocial immortality, which is to say having children to carry on one's name and to inherit one's characteristics as well as one's possessions, is universal. There are still reported cases in China (where only one child per family is allowed by law) of female infants being killed at birth so that further opportunity for a male heir exists. Portable abortion clinics are said to dot the Chinese countryside providing abortions of the female fetus. Can this be other than human longing for one's name to remain through the progeny of male offspring, living on through one's children?

As more and more ways of having children later and later in life are developed, and more methods are made available for artificial conditions of conception, we only further manifest our worship of youth and of technology. For men in our society, having children after the age of 50 has become a growing trend. Celebrities Jack Nicholson and Warren Beatty are but two of many whose desire for immortality and worship of youth (fear of death), might be explained by the fathering of children during their 50's. One well-known actor noted that fathering children over the age of 50 fosters feelings of immortality.

Unlike men, women in their late 40's and early 50's run out of biological chances for immortality, although even that condition is being altered through the process of artificial insemination. A 52-year-old grandmother recently gave birth to twins after having been artificially inseminated. Yet the following is still true for women with regard to issues of death, denial and biosocial immortality:

> Menopause reawakens the horror of the body, the utter bankruptcy of the body as a viable causa-sui project . . . woman is reminded in the most forceful way that she is an animal thing; menopause is a sort of "animal birthday" that specifically marks the physical career of degeneration. It is like nature imposing a definite physical milestone on the person, putting up a wall and saying, "You are going no further into life now, you are going toward the end to the absolute determinism of death." As men don't have such animal birthdays, such specific markers of a physical kind, they don't usually experience another stark discrediting of the body as a causa-sui project. . . . But the woman is less fortunate, she is put in the position of having all at once to catch up psychologically with the physical facts of life. To paraphrase Goethe's aphorism, death

doesn't keep knocking on the door only to be ignored (as men ignore aging) but kicks it in to show himself full face.[4]

Ironically our own technological successes with contraception have removed some of the biological or biosocial opportunities. As Dr. Rollo May noted in his book *Love and Will*, we have "shifted man's death-defying sexual instincts from procreation to performance." Our obsessive coupling and uncoupling suggested to May that Americans have frantically turned to sexual titillation for deliverance from the anxiety of death. It is death, not sex, May argue, that is the basic cause of man's psychic disorder. "The clamor of sex drowns out the ever-waiting presence of death . . . because death is the symbol of ultimate impotence and finiteness. . . . What would we see," asks May, if we "cut through our obsession with sex . . . that we must die."[5]

One is reminded of the movie *Moonstruck* in which the character Rose asks why men chase women. Her answer is that men chase women because men fear death. The recently-revealed sexual excesses of President John F. Kennedy become more understandable in the context of Dr. May's theory and Rose's philosophical questioning.

It is well known that the Kennedy family has been plagued with death, both tragic and premature. First there was John F. Kennedy's older brother, Joe Jr., who was shot down during a World War II bombing mission. His death was followed closely by that of sister Kathleen, who died along with her husband in a plane crash. What may have been one of the most poignant moments of John Kennedy's life was later described by an aide who had informed him of his sister's death. In his sorrow, said the aide, Kennedy sat alone, weeping, as he listened to a recording of their favorite Irish tune.

Nor was John Kennedy a stranger to personal death. Having barely survived the crash of his PT boat during the war, he suffered recurring bouts of a perilous illness that was later diagnosed as Addison's Disease. Seven times he lay so near death that the last rites of the Catholic Church were administered to him. His deep preoccupation with death led Kennedy to confide in his pal, George Smathers, that "the point is to live every day as if it's going to be your last on earth. That's what I'm going to do." From then on, said Smathers, "girls went in and out of Jack's bed in such numbers that he often neglected to learn their names, referring to them the next morning as merely 'sweetie' or 'kiddo'."[6]

If not through sexual prowess and procreation, escape from the terrors of physical death may be sought in the teachings of religion. Nearly all major world religions promise an afterlife in some form, hence religion's timeless appeal. Many religions also embrace the concept of transcendence, a metaphysical state beyond the bounds of human existence as we know them to a point where we are, in simple terms, at one with the universe. Whether physical or spiritual, our longing to be a part of eternity cannot be refuted. At some level we all aspire to live forever and it is religion that offers the greatest hope of doing so.[7]

For some that search for immortality may be directed toward nature. Nature as an ongoing, immortal state has been accepted by numerous cultures over the centuries including that of Native Americans who felt that death simply meant returning to Mother Earth. Robert J. Lifton spent time in Japan following World War II. He noted that among the Japanese, the return of the cherry blossoms after the bombing of Hiroshima and Nagasaki was seen as the victory of nature over the modern means of destructive technology.[8]

When Korean Flight 007 was shot down, relatives of the dead spread chrysanthemums on the waters where those killed in the crash may have fallen, chrysanthemums being only one of several symbols of longevity and endurance acknowledged among Eastern cultures.

And then there is creative immortality. William Faulkner described creative immortality when he accepted the Nobel Prize for literature in 1949. "This," he said, "is the artist's way of scribbling, 'Kilroy was here,' on the wall of the final and irrevocable oblivion through which he someday must pass."

Most of us will never be immortalized for our creative contributions to society. What we pass on will likely be nothing more than a family keepsake. But the quilt, the hope chest, the painted dishes are every bit as much an attempt at immortality as are the initials we carve in fresh cement as children, of the graffiti sprayed across decaying urban areas by society's unacknowledged—verification that we once lived. Frederick Perls described four layers of neurotic human behavior, the fourth and most baffling of which was the fear-of-death layer. And that layer, observed Ernest Becker, "was the layer of our true and basic animal anxieties, which causes us terror that we carry around unacknowledged in our heart."[9]

We know that, in the end, money will not spare us from death, nor will possessions nor talents nor age nor youth nor family nor social standing. But so long as we avoid and deny and distance the anxieties raised by the reality that we are going to die, death will continue to be the troublesome taboo that sex was in Freud's age, lying repressed in our unconscious where it exacts from us an intolerable emotional recompense.

Chapter Three

We Are All Terminal, Aren't We?

While I thought I was learning how to live, I was learning how to die.

—Leonardo da Vinci

A significant element of our death denial has to do with the fear of falling victim to terminal illness. Through direct experience or our own imaginings, we may be terrorized by the prospect of lying helplessly immersed in pain, as the terminally ill often are. Even more than the physical suffering, we may dread the loss of dignity that lack of choice embodies. What choices, after all, are offered to the dying—choices in where to die, in the company of whom, or when and under what conditions death will occur?

In our guts (head-on-the-pillow at night), we know we are no less than mortal. One prayer of childhood even includes a reference to such knowledge, stating . . . "if I should die before I wake." Yet the utter terror evoked by the reality of such a prospect compels us, even as adults, to turn to a form of childish indulgence, that of pretending. We pretend that if we believe death does not exist, it will simply go away.

Have you ever pretended that you were dying by asking yourself the question, "If I had six months to live, what would I do?" How different would our daily lives be if we assumed each morning that we only had only a few more todays? What if we actually believed what we know to be true, that we are all terminal? Perhaps then the answer to that question, "If I had six months to live, what would I do," would be more like that of those who have been given a death sentence. Their response most often is, "I would do just what I have been doing, if only I had the chance to do it all ONE MORE TIME."

Put yourself in their place for a moment. Imagine that you are ill, very ill, so ill that you are certain you are dying. Someone enters your sickroom, there to confirm what you already know. Who would you want that person to be—your doctor, a friend, your closest confidant? Would you want their answers to your questions to be honest ones? Who else would you want to know that you were dying? Would you want to tell those individuals yourself, or let someone else do that for you?

Now imagine that instead of you it is someone you love who is dying. You must go to see this person. What will you say? What will be the response? Should you be forthright or evasive if asked for the truth? Should you be thinking of what you'd want the person to say to you if you were dying, or simply listen?

The first time I saw my mother following her diagnosis, I wondered what I would say to her. I needn't have. She was standing in her kitchen waiting for me, my plane having been delayed by heavy fog. I was shocked at how young and beautiful her profile was. Then she turned and said, "I'm so glad you came." Her eyes were filled with terror but her voice was calm. You could see death in her look.

She handed me a pamphlet on ovarian cancer in which she had underlined, in her trademark purple ink, a few key passages. They dealt with how soon the cancer had been detected as far as survival was concerned. In her case that had not been soon enough. What she was telling me was that she knew the hopelessness of her condition and she wanted me to know too, so that I could help her deal realistically with it.

But for all the times I had read and heard about that defense mechanism known as denial, when it stared me in the face I looked away. I wasn't listening. Only later, after my mother had died, and I came across that pamphlet lying on her kitchen counter did I understand what she had been trying to convey. What must she have thought of the wallet that lay partially unwrapped nearby— a Christmas present I had given her just weeks before she died?

Denial on the part of loved ones not able to confront impending realities, a medical force largely trained to equate death with failure, and the belief held by many in our technologically driven society that there is always a cure for everything out there somewhere—all conspire to dilute the truth of death.

The difficulty in choosing whether or not to pursue treatment can only be imagined by those of us not faced with it. How much more difficult that choice becomes if there is no opportunity for dialogue between the terminally ill and their loved ones. Already emotionally isolated, perhaps angry or depressed, those labeled terminal face far more than just the prospect of physical pain. They face the prospect of feeling that they are alone. When told of her condition, my mother initially adopted a stoic approach, reasoning that heroic-extraordinary measures to prolong her life were futile. After the hospital staff arranged for her to meet with a fellow ovarian cancer patient who was in remission following chemotherapy treatment, she changed her mind and submitted to chemotherapy treatments too. Perhaps that was part of her effort at denial.

Even more dreaded than the prospect of death itself may be the fear of not being heard. The dying may have a lot they would like to say, but the opportunity for expressing their wishes and worries is often denied them. Part of what they might say includes the following:

- I know how sick I am, don't lie to me.
- We need to talk about what's really going on here.
- Your pretending only makes it harder for me to share what I'm going through.
- I don't have time to waste on mindless banter.
- Yes, I feel anger about my condition but it's not meant to be personal so please don't take it that way.
- When I am depressed, as I will be, just hold my hand, or be near. There are ways to tell me you care without speaking when I haven't the strength to listen.
- I may raise an issue that makes you uncomfortable (such as about my funeral or will, or what will happen after I die). Please try to get through it somehow. Don't put me off with, "We'll talk about it later."
- If at some point I should request your permission to die, grant it if you are able. My asking signals that I am ready.
- Most of all, don't pretend that I am no longer here. Don't talk with others in my presence as though I don't exist. Don't take away the only dignity left me, that feeling that I still have some choice. Then I will truly feel alone and abandoned.

No one who has walked into the room of a dying person would deny how utterly draining it can be. Gazing at a wasted frame threaded with tubes, monitored by machines, emitting odors of decomposition, one is overcome with a sense of fear and vulnerability related to one's own mortality. I remember my uncle walking past my mother's hospital room and then coming back. He had not recognized her, or perhaps he didn't want to admit to himself that he did.

"I didn't realize that the chemotherapy makes them lose their eyebrows and eyelashes too," he said as he gazed at her in disbelief. Just then a young intern gently pulled my uncle aside. He explained that because hearing is the last sense lost, it is important not to say anything you wouldn't wish the person to hear.

What the dying want to hear depends a great deal upon their individual outlook. Just as each of us approaches living in our own original way, so too do we cope with death in a personal way. Whatever the coping mechanisms may be, something we all need to hear during the process is gentle reinforcement of the truth. Only then can we come to terms with the inevitable. It doesn't mean that one must remove the patient's hope, but it does mean facing up to what will realistically be the final outcome. The following passage from *Anna Karenina* is telling:

Death, the inevitable end of everything, confronted him for the first time with irresistible force. And death which was close to his beloved brother . . . was not so far away as it had hitherto seemed to him. It was in himself too—he felt it. If not today, then tomorrow, if not tomorrow, then 30 years hence . . . at that moment both of them were preoccupied with the same thought—Nikolai's illness and approaching death—which put everything else out of their minds. But neither dared speak of it, and consequently, everything they said, since it did not express what they really thought, rang false.[1]

Dealing with the truth may trigger anger and resentment. Anger is not an emotion that is easily dealt with, especially in the context of death. Anger may further serve to damage lines of communication already strained. The important thing to remember, regardless of how difficult, is that we must keep the dialogue going.

At several points during her illness my mother said to me, "I'm so glad you know as much about death as you do, and that you can talk with me about it. Most people can't." One evening we watched a TV version of *The Shadowbox*, the story of a group of terminally ill people struggling in a variety of ways to face death. Afterwards she asked me what I thought and I said that I found it to be a realistic depiction of how difficult dying really is, just how angry you'd be.

That night I awoke with severe stomach pains and spent most of the time until morning in the bathroom. I kept seeing my mother standing over the kitchen sink, trying to wash down her medications with orange juice, only to have it all come back up again. Once, when she had sensed me observing her, she had gotten angry. "You've never really been sick, have you?" she asked.

When I told her about my stomach pains I felt guilty, knowing how minor they were compared to what she was suffering. She just looked at me and said again, "You've never really been sick, have you?" And then she said, "You're lucky and I am glad for you."

What she didn't say, but what I knew was that she understood the source of my discomfort the night before. During one of our talks some days earlier, she had recalled taking care of my nephew, Eric, then four or five years old, while his parents were away. He had complained that his stomach hurt. She knew it was because he missed his mother. What she said to me was, "I wish someone loved me the way that child loves his mother." Thankfully, before she died, she knew that someone did.

But no amount of love will ultimately eradicate the fact that death is going to occur. When a 19-year-old leukemia patient named Eric Lund was asked by a group of nurses to explain what he thought they could do to help the dying deal with that fact, he responded, "Don't ever take away their hope." He understood that the wonderful and remarkable thing about hope is its ability to keep a dying person alive longer. If that hope includes an impending wedding, a birth, an anniversary or gradua- tion, some indescribable something seems to infuse the patient with the renewed strength to witness it. Once the event has occurred, death may follow quickly, giving rise to an interesting question of just how much choice the dying exercise over when they die.

With or without such bursts of hope, the time comes when the terminally ill individual in effect says, "I'm ready now, not necessarily that I want to die, but I am ready." When our mother conveyed to us that she was ready, we asked her if she would like to go home to die. She said yes. Her oncologist advised us that her life would be shortened (possibly by weeks) if treatment were discontinued. Having said that, his voice broke as he added, "What you are doing for your mother is a wonderful thing." We were no different than any other family faced with such circum- stances. Death doesn't offer easy choices to the dying, nor to those who love them.

Although it was not an option for our mother— because there was no hospice near her home—many fami- lies now select such a form of alternative care. Hospice is often seen as a way to achieve death with dignity, free of unnecessary pain and intrusive medical procedures. The word hospice means "a house of refuge . . . for a traveler, especially one conducted by a religious order." The first hospice, St. Christopher's, was established in London,

England in 1902. Since then the hospice concept has spread worldwide.

Only those who are believed to have six or fewer months to live are accepted into most U.S. hospice programs. Admission signals the exchange of traditional medical treatment for only that necessary to reduce and control pain and discomfort. This is referred to as palliative care.

The hospice philosophy is based on the belief that the first step in helping someone achieve death with dignity is to eliminate as much pain as possible. One attempt at that, made in the early days of hospice, was serving patients something called a "Brompton Cocktail." It consisted of their favorite drink laced with adequate amounts of painkiller, usually liquid morphine. Supplying pain-killing drugs in liquid form eliminated the agony of injections and allowed patients a source of pleasure at the same time.

Hospice has been criticized for encouraging drug addiction by providing as much painkiller as the patient required rather than the X cc's every X hours. The idea of consuming alcohol was also frowned upon by some. So too was allowing hospice patients to smoke when many were dying of cancer.

One hospice worker described assisting in just such a case, that of an elderly gentleman dying of cancer who came into the program literally kicking and screaming obscenities. Once his pain-control needs had been assessed and implemented, he was asked what else could be done to make him comfortable. All he wanted, he said, was to be able to drink wine and smoke cigars. His requests were granted. He died peacefully a few weeks later.

That man's wish for escape from the suffering and futility of protracted and possible hopeless medical treatment, into a world where he could indulge his greatest, although unhealthy pleasures, gave him what hospice strives for—death with dignity, meaning death with choice about, and control over, one's final days—a peaceful exit. Hospice care sometimes means a shorter survival time due to the withdrawal of active treatment, but that shortened survival time is meant to be of the highest quality possible.

In addition to meeting the physical needs of patients through pain control and alleviation, hospice strives to meet patients' emotional needs. Those emotional needs may cover everything, including where the person wishes to die and whom, if anyone, he or she wishes to be present when death occurs.

Most hospice facilities include rooms for patients within a hospital, but in no other way are they part of the traditional hospital setting. Instead they are organized and arranged like the rooms in one's home, with cheerful bedrooms, a sitting area and guestrooms for family members or friends who wish to remain overnight. Those hospice patients who choose to, and are able, may stay at home where the same hospice volunteer and professional help is provided to them and their families.

There are no restrictions on visiting hours in most hospice facilities. Children and pets are allowed. So are family events such as birthday parties, weddings and graduation ceremonies. In cases where the patient cannot participate outside the hospice setting, the events, if possible, are brought to them.

One hospice volunteer described her home visits to a middle-aged woman who was dying of cancer. Each time she would show me family photos, said the volunteer. "I didn't know the people, but it gave her so much pleasure to tell me about them." Another told of caring for a great Dane dog that was brought to the room of a young leukemia victim at the hospice. "When she opened her eyes for the last time," said the volunteer, "she got to see her dog."

A 10-year-old child who died at home with hospice care requested that his body not ever be transported by ambulance again, because so often during his illness he had had to ride in one. In the early dawn hours following his death, hospice staff members drove his body to the funeral home in a station wagon. "The sun was just coming up along the lakeshore," said the nurse who had cared for him. "He would have liked that, he wouldn't have been afraid."

That same hospice worker told of a phone call she received from a man, distraught over the behavior of his dying wife. "She doesn't love me anymore," he lamented, "She keeps pushing me away." The hospice worker reassured him that his wife, contrary to not loving him, was signaling him that she was very near death, by cathecting from him.

Cathect comes from the Greek word, cathexis, meaning the withholding or withdrawal of emotions and attachments by the dying from those around them. This emotional withdrawal or closing down usually signals that death is imminent.

When we were preparing to take my mother home from the hospital that final time, I remember approaching her bed, wishing to hug her. "Don't get too close," she said, holding me at arm's length, "don't get too close."

Loved ones may understandably misinterpret what is happening during cathexis. It may seem to them that the dying person no longer loves or cares for them, when in truth it is necessary for the dying person to cathect in order to bear the separation from everyone and everything that has been dear to them.

As with cathexis, the matter of so-called unfinished business requires that the terminally ill be carefully listened to. At those times when they care to speak of it, give them your full attention, and then simply do whatever you can that they ask. That may include helping to make funeral plans, assisting with last good-byes, dealing with regrets and omissions, disposing of personal property or possessions, or whatever else.

It didn't dawn on me initially that when my mother asked me to wash all the windows on her huge Victorian house, inside and out, in January, that there could be a good reason. But having done so without hesitation I realized that she knew friends and relatives would gather at the house before and after the funeral, and in her Martha Stewart-like lifetime pursuit of domestic perfection, for which she was renowned, she wanted those windows clean.

On the morning of the day my mother died, she looked at me with her penetrating black eyes and announced, "We're going." When I asked her where, she just repeated, "We're going."

With that, she got out of bed and walked into the dining room that she had so tastefully decorated to emphasize its stained-glass windows. She sat at the head of her prized French provincial dining room table, where a month earlier she had insisted that we not include her in a holiday family picture. Then she moved on to the kitchen and once again seated herself at the table where we had shared so many conversations over cups of Swedish coffee. Her last stop was her own bed where she lay down and fully intended to stay. It was only the need for oxygen that took her reluctantly back to the hospital bed set up for her in the living room. Twelve hours later she was dead.

Recently an acquaintance whose wife was dying of cancer asked me if I thought having gone through the experience of caring for a terminally ill person once would provide better understanding of what to do the next time. "I've never done this," he offered. "I wish I knew more."

We all wish we knew more, and at the same time we

hope and wish that we'll never have to know it at all. But based on reality, formulating a perspective, a viewpoint, an approach to the possibility that it might just as well be you or me lying in that bed under the sentence of life's most dreaded diagnosis would seem prudent.

As a society we haven't yet reached the point where we can openly talk about death. When asked about the topic for a recent, nationwide focus group study on issues of death and dying, participants' initial response was that they found death too depressing, too sad, bad luck, too far in the future or something that they were too busy to talk about.[2]

Death is depressing for limitless numbers of reasons, not the least of which is that ultimately we haven't the ability to prevent it. A mature approach to death begins with the acknowledgment of the fact that indeed we are all terminal. Acceptance of that certainty generates necessary consideration of just how much control we care to exert with regard to the circumstances of our own death. Do we have the right to choose a peaceful exit, death with dignity, the good or well death? And if the answer is yes, then how do we secure it for ourselves and for those we love? Denial or dialogue, disengagement or serious discussion—each of us must determine which it will be—for we are all terminal, aren't we?

Chapter Four

Who Should Live?
Who Should Die?
Who Should Decide?

Nancy Cruzan, now 32, has done nothing for the past seven years. She has not hugged her mother or gazed out the window or played with her nieces. She has neither laughed nor wept . . . nor spoken a word . . . she has lain still for so long that her hands have curled into claws. . . . "She would hate to be like this," says her mother Joyce, "it has taken a long time to accept she wasn't getting better."[1]

      In January of 1983, Nancy Cruzan was found in an icy field, the victim of a car crash that caused her to nearly suffocate. The rescue squad that revived her after some 45 minutes had no legal right to consider the likelihood of her having sustained brain damage due to lack of oxygen. Their task was to resuscitate, which they did. If Nancy had been wearing a DNR—Do Not Resuscitate—bracelet, which she was not, the duty of the rescue squad was still to take every possible step to save her life.

      By the time Nancy Cruzan reached the emergency room, her family had been notified of the accident and was waiting. Shocked at her appearance, her sister Christie later recalled that the only thing she recognized about Nancy were her socks.

Almost immediately, Nancy's parents were asked to make major decisions regarding her care. One decision was whether to allow a feeding tube to be placed in Nancy's stomach because she could not swallow liquid or food. Having no knowledge of the extent of their daughter's brain damage at that time, the Cruzans opted for the procedure.

Each day in this country a family like the Cruzans is presented with such ominous decisions regarding issues of life support for someone they love. As medical technology advances, the choices will only become more difficult by the very nature of their complexity. Thinking and talking about such issues does not seem to be something that most of us want to do. Perhaps we assume that nothing like what happened to the Cruzans will happen to us. Or maybe we think that it isn't possible to make such decisions until, and if, the time comes. How does one ever really make such choices?

Human choice? Who are we humans to choose between life and death? Is that not the power of providence? And if not the power of providence, then who among us shall decide—family, clergy, legal authorities, medical personnel, ethicists, who? And on what do we base our decision? Ours is a society that has yet to agree upon when life begins. How then can we arbitrarily say it has ended?

Webster's Dictionary defines death as "the cessation of all vital functions without capability of resuscitation," and defines being dead as "deprived of life—opposed to alive and living; reduced to that state of being in which the organs of motion and life have irrevocably ceased to perform their functions." Years ago when someone stopped breathing for a reasonable period of time they were considered to be dead. Tests to make sure of death included tickling the nose with a feather or holding a mirror near the mouth to see if vapor formed. In a less scientific age there were, no doubt, a few mistaken pronouncements of death. As we know today, measurable signs of life such as breathing and heartbeat may cease for several minutes before recurring and numerous cases of such "near deaths" have been documented.

In the United States, legal determination of death was first derived from the so-called Harvard Criteria, published in 1968 by an ad hoc committee of the Harvard Medical School. The list included:

1. Inability of the patient to breathe when taken off a respirator for a period of four minutes.
2. A total lack of responses to any external stimuli.
3. The absence of all basic brain stem reflexes (swallowing, coughing, yawning), i.e., "brain death."

Under the Harvard criteria, tests to determine death were made every 24 hours. The heart and lungs were supported artificially. Diagnostic tests such as C.A.T. scans were used to determine the extent of brain damage sustained.

While the American Medical Association continued to accept cessation of functions of the brain as only one criterion of death, the American Bar Association, in 1975, declared that: "for all legal purposes, a human body with irrevocable cessation of total brain functions according to usual and customary standards of medical practice shall be considered dead."[2] That was the same year that 21-year-old Karen Ann Quinlan slipped into a coma from which she never emerged.

After being kept alive artificially by hospital technology for a year, Ms. Quinlan's family appealed to the New Jersey court system to allow her to be taken off the machines. The court agreed to do so. What shocked the

world was not the court's decision so much as the fact that
Karen Ann Quinlan, unaided by respirators, continued to
live—or at least to survive—until 1983.

Her youthful heart and lungs were strong—strong
enough to continue for many years. The problem was that
her delicate brain tissue, briefly deprived of oxygen, was
permanently damaged. As doctors described it, she might
go on breathing, "but she'll never wake up."

Here is the "monster incarnate"—the technology
we rely on to deny death its due—the same technology
that can save us—can also imprison us in an escape-proof
shell of permanent vegetative bondage. We become, as in
the horror pictures, "the living dead." There are over
10,000 such prisoners of living death in this country today.

The Karen Ann Quinlan case embodied that mon-
strous technological horror, but it also signified the beginning of a definition of death based on loss of cognitive-
sapient abilities rather than just simple reflexive brain
functions. This became known as the "brain death" definition as opposed to the earlier "heart-lung" definition out-
lined in the Harvard Criteria.

Courts ruled in Quinlan's case that respirators
could be removed if the family, attending physician and a
hospital ethics committee concured that there was no reasonable chance of recovering cognitive-sapient abilities. In
other words, these patients will never again be aware of
who they are and where they are, nor will they ever again
be able to think and reason—the very things that make us
human.

The American Bar Association, the American
Medical Association and the Uniform Law Committee all
adopted a Uniform Determination of Death Act in the
early 1980's, which stated:

An individual who has sustained either, (1) irreversible cessa-
tion of circulatory and respiratory functions or (2) irreversible
cessation of all functions of the entire brain including the
brain stem, is dead. Determination of death must be made in
accordance with accepted medical standards.[3]

So with the Quinlan case and the Uniform
Determination of Death Act, accepted by both medical and
legal authority, why is there still a problem in declaring
someone dead?

Over 3,000 years ago Greek society faced the same
stultifying questions with regard to death. Greek philosophy taught that there was both a proper time and a proper
way to die. The Greeks came up with the word euthanasia—*eu* meaning easy, plus *thanatos* meaning death.
Thanatos was the Greek god of death.

Webster's Dictionary defines euthanasia as both
"the good or easy death or means of inducing one," and as
the "act or practice of painlessly putting to death persons
suffering from incurable and distressing diseases." The
Greek concept of euthanasia is not as simply defined,
understood, nor accepted in 20th-century life because we
define euthanasia in several ways.

There is voluntary euthanasia, in which the person,
knowing he or she wants to die, asks to do so. Involuntary
euthanasia is quite the opposite. In this case, the person is
not capable of expressing a wish to die. The decision, if
made, is made by someone else.

Passive euthanasia, or the withholding of treatment
of life-support, is commonly practiced and rather widely
accepted. Someone may ask to be removed from a respirator or not to be resuscitated or operated on again, knowing
that the decision will result in death.

Most religious believers do not object to this. They see it as life
coming naturally to its end. So passive euthanasia is not tech-
nically defined as assisted suicide. In most places it is now

sanctioned by legislators and widely practiced by doctors (though difficulty still arises if the patient is comatose and cannot say what he wants).[4]

Active euthanasia is not as palatable for many. Active euthanasia is the hastening of death, not by withholding efforts, but rather through administration or prescription of drugs. Under most circumstances, this can be interpreted as a crime.

There might be difficulty determining whether a lethal dosage of drugs was prescribed simply to control pain or whether it was intentionally administered to cause death to occur. It might also be difficult to determine who administered the dosage and under what circumstances.

Unlike euthanasia, doctor-assisted suicide provides the individual who wishes to die only the means for doing so. It is the patient who administers the lethal dosage to him or herself. Jack Kevorkian is probably the best-known practitioner of physician-assisted suicide, though he has colleagues in other parts of the world. One such colleague is Philip Nitsche, an Australian physician, who provides a laptop-computer to patients with instructions on the computer screen for how to inject themselves. A machine attached to the computer administers the lethal drugs.

Kevorkian has said all along that he only wants to offer the terminally ill a painless and dignified alternative. He was charged with first-degree murder for aiding in the suicide of an Alzheimer's patient, Janet Adkins.

The 54-year-old Mrs. Adkins contacted Kevorkian for help in taking her own life after hearing of his suicide van. She, her husband, Ronald, and a close friend flew to Detroit where they met with Kevorkian. His suicide procedure was discussed by the foursome over dinner. The next day Janet entered the suicide van while her husband waited at a nearby motel. She pressed a button, which changed the sedative flowing intravenously into her arm to a deadly chemical, potassium chloride. Within minutes, Janet Adkins was dead.

Janet Adkins was a member of the Hemlock Society, which supports the legalization of assisted suicides for the terminally ill. She had favored suicide since being told that she suffered from the incurable disease known as Alzheimer's. After trying experimental drugs and counseling with her minister and her sons, she contacted Dr. Kevorkian. Following her death, Janet Adkins' husband said of his wife: "they had been grieving for year . . . but she was the one who kept everyone going up until the last." Kevorkian said he was trying to knock the medical profession into accepting its responsibilities, including assisting their patients with death.

Dr. Kevorkian was tried and acquitted for his role in assisting Janet Adkins to take her life. After advising two more seriously ill people on how to die (both committed suicide after seeking out Kevorkian for information on how to do so), Kevorkian's medical license was revoked.

Kevorkian was acquitted for the fourth time in the assisted suicides of 58-year-old Marjorie Wantz and 43-year-old Sherry Miller. Mrs. Wantz suffered from constant pain despite 10 operations for genital ailments. The night before her death, Mrs Wantz said she would use a gun to take her life but she didn't know how to load one.

Immobilized by multiple sclerosis, Sherry Miller left a message which described how she sat in a chair for a year, not being able to move and being dependent on other people. "It's not living," she said, "it's just existing. And who would like to do that?"

The Jack Kevorkian case was viewed by many as a potential "watershed in the right to die." Some physicians felt it would compel them to extreme measures in keeping their terminally ill patients alive, at the risk of being charged with a crime. Yet the concept of assisted suicide seems to be gaining public support. The Hemlock Society's recent poll, conducted by the Roper Organization, found that 64% of Americans favor the idea of medically assisted suicide. The society's membership has doubled to 33,000 in the last five years. Derrick Humphreys, the Hemlock Society's founder, has said of Kevorkian's case, that it was not death with dignity to die in the back of a camper, having travelled several thousand miles from home to do so.

Humphreys, who assisted his first wife in her suicide following the diagnosis of terminal breast cancer, has written two books on the subject. The more recent *Final Exit* was on the *New York Times* bestseller list for months. The majority of its buyers were middle-aged people who said they feared the prospect of a prolonged and possibly painful illness. Many of them were said to have secured supplies of drugs recommended by Humphreys for that final exit.

For over 20 years the Netherlands has legally sanctioned both euthanasia and physician-assisted suicide, without drawing legal and ethical lines of demarcation between the two. As long as a physician obeys four guidelines regarding assisted suicide or euthanasia, he or she will not be prosecuted. The four guidelines are:
1. The patient must be a mentally competent adult.
2. The patient must require euthanasia voluntarily, consistently and repeatedly over a reasonable period of time.
3. The patient must be suffering intolerably with no prospect of relief, although the disease need not be terminal.
4. The doctor must consult with another physician not involved in the case.

Because of widespread concern over possible abuses of physician-assisted suicide and euthanasia, the Dutch government launched a study to determine what really went on between doctors and their patients. The initial study was done in 1990, followed by another in 1995. Both were supported by the Royal Dutch Medical Association. Doctors who took part were granted immunity from possible prosecution.

Over 500 doctors were interviewed for the study with questionnaires sent to over 6,000 others. It was found that, in general, Dutch doctors received a large number of requests for help in dying (8,900 in 1990 and 9,700 in 1995). But they responded to only some of these. Of the roughly 130,000 deaths in the Netherlands in 1990, the study estimated from physician interviews and questionnaires that 2,300 deaths were a result of euthanasia, or about 1.8 percent. Another 400 deaths were a result of assisted suicide, about 0.3 percent.[5]

One of the arguments against the legalization of physician-assisted suicide and euthanasia has been that lives will be taken without consent, not because the dying person asked to die but rather because those in charge felt it was time. If the dying patient cannot make a determination regarding his or her wishes with respect to resuscitation, the family may be asked to do so. An example of this was the case of Oliver Wanglie in Minnesota.

Wanglie, 87, was asked by the hospital to make a decision to remove his wife, Helga, 87, from a respirator. Doctors and her family argued that she had been in a persistent vegetative state since suffering a heart attack that interrupted blood flow to her brain.

In the first case where a medical agency asked a judge over family members' objections, to take action that would likely result in the patient's death, two doctors testified that keeping Helga Wanglie on a respirator is "inappropriate medicine" because she cannot be cured and her condition is irreversible. Oliver Wanglie argued that he wanted his wife kept on the respirator in hope that a miracle might occur and she would recover. Wanglie argued that as long as his wife's heart was beating she was still alive, and that she would not want to be taken off life support. Helga Wanglie died before a final ruling was given by the courts.

The Helga Wanglie case represents an ethical and moral dilemma that will haunt our future. By the year 2000, almost 10 percent of America's population was 65 or older. It is estimated that up to 30 percent of Medicare costs for the elderly are spent during the last years of their lives. It is a fact that 13 percent of the elderly receive 82 percent of all Medicare spending.

What our nation faces is the question of how we will allocate resources. Will those working to support health care systems for the elderly be able to meet the demands? Who can be kept alive, for how long and at what cost? How will the Helga Wanglie cases be decided— by the courts, by family members, by doctors? And what if they cannot agree? The United States Supreme Court ruled in 1997 that it is up to individual states to determine where they stand on physician-assisted suicide. Currently, Oregon is the only state to have passed a law allowing physician-assisted suicide.

Under Oregon's law, a terminally ill patient who is a resident of the state and who wishes to die, would have to make both an oral and a written request for legal medication to his or her doctor. The first oral request would then be followed by consultation with a second doctor. A 15-day interval would follow before any medication was prescribed.

The state of Oregon forbids active euthanasia. As a safeguard against it, the law further requires that written requests for the right-to-die be witnessed by at least one person who has no interest in inheriting or otherwise benefiting from the death. At least 48 hours must pass between the written request to die and the death itself.

In California, attempted suicide gets you a three-day stay at a mental institution. In the state of New York, at one time anyone who announced an intention to die through self-inflicted starvation was force-fed.

A New York group called Partnership for Caring, which does not take an official stand on assisted suicide and euthanasia, says that calls to its office have increased from 200-300 to 5,000 per week since the deaths of former President Richard M. Nixon, and former First Lady Jacqueline Kennedy-Onassis. Both Nixon and Onassis had prepared advance directives which included, in the case of Onassis, the wish to die at home, possibly at a self-designated time of her choosing. Said Karen Orloff-Kaplan, executive director of Partnership for Caring:

The question of how we spend the final chapter of our lives is very important. Whether people talk about it or not, it's on everyone's mind.[6]

How will we spend the final chapters of our lives? Jacqueline Kennedy-Onassis died in her 5th Avenue apartment surrounded by her own things. She chose how, and perhaps to some degree when she would die. What made a political death sentence acceptable to Socrates was the fact that he chose to impose it. He drank the hemlock in an act that was considered to be the ultimate expression of control in Greek society.

Is choice regarding when and how we die more important than prolongation of life under any circumstances? The U.S. Supreme Court ruled in the Nancy Cruzan case that if a person's wishes with regard to life-sustaining treatment are clearly known, then life-support systems may be removed. But because the then 25-year-old Nancy Cruzan had not signed a living will declaring her wish to be allowed to die should she fall victim to such a persistent vegetative state, prior to her accident, the state of Missouri (her legal guardian) and not her family had the right to limit decisions such as removal of the feeding tube.

Following the high court's ruling, Ms. Cruzan's family was able to gain testimony from additional witnesses who stated that Nancy would not want to be kept alive artificially. That testimony was enough for the Circuit Court Judge Charles E. Teel Jr. to rule that in the U.S. Supreme Court criteria Cruzan's case applied and that the feeding tube could be removed. Nancy Cruzan died 12 days later of "shock due to dehydration due to severe head injury."

At her funeral, Nancy Cruzan's father, Joe Cruzan, had this to say:

Today, as the protesters' signs say, we give Nancy the gift of death—an unconditional gift of love that sets her free from this twisted body that no longer serves her, a gift I know she will treasure above all others, a gift of freedom.[7]

Nancy Cruzan's family, in their struggle to set her free, also freed millions of others concerned about being kept alive artificially in a persistent vegetative state. The U.S. Supreme Court ruled in the Cruzan case that "a person whose wishes are clearly known has a constitutionally protected right to reject life-sustaining treatment." That decision led to a pervasive interest in living wills and durable power-of-attorney for health care.

Such documents now must be explained to all hospital patients according to federal law. The practice of discussing with one's physician or close family members what one's wishes would be in the face of being kept alive by machines has also spread. According to Nancy Cruzan's father Joe, interest in living wills has increased 500-fold since her case received national attention, speaking to the legacy that her death represents.

But can we face tragedy and accept its random inexplicability within the bounds of our technology-worshipping, death-denying culture? What is our definition of death? Where do we draw the line? Is death with dignity, a peaceful exit, the easy or well death of euthanasia all we want? Or must even our deaths be somehow productive?

Consider the moral dilemma created by Anna, born two months prematurely with multiple birth defects. She had no eyes, part of her brain was missing, she suffered from hydrocephalus (a severe swelling of the head), and in addition to a nasal obstruction, she had a cleft palate. Part of her forearm was missing and she had extra fingers.

A regional right-to-life group, the Family Life League, complained to public agencies that the child was not being fed and parental orders to the staff were not to fondle her. Shortly after being moved to another hospital Anna died.

According to at least two geneticists, her defects ruled out survival. According to hospital sources, attempts were made to feed her under an order stating "feed as tolerated." The hospital said there was no order restricting the staff to fondle the child. No heroic-extraordinary measures were taken, because, said her doctor: "Her abnormalities were not compatible with survival. I didn't deem heroic measures proper and the parents didn't want it."

After an Illinois Department of Children and Family Services investigation Anna's parents and the hospital were exonerated of any wrongdoing. Family Life League official Laura Canning, who called the authorities about the case, said she still thought the parents and the hospital were guilty.

When nine-year-old Alyssa Plum died, after unsuccessful lung transplants from both of her parents, medical ethicists questioned whether the shortage of organs from cadavers might not be pushing medical technology further and faster than it should go and whether parents are asked to give too much to save their children. Referred to by one physician as an "ethical bog," the question raised by medical ethicists in Alyssa's situation is what restrictions should be placed upon parents' rights to donate organs to their children? And would such restrictions lessen a parent's guilt or help in their decision making?

What of the couple who chose to conceive a child in the hopes that that infant's bone marrow could save the life of an older sibling? That is what Mary and Abe Ayala did. Unable to locate a living donor of bone marrow for their 17-year-old daughter, Annissa, they found a perfect match in Annissa's infant sister who was born to save her from the ravages of myelogeneous leukemia. A similar case was recently reported—this time where a newborn son provided blood as a cure for his older sister.

The ethical question of how much should be asked from the parents for the sake of the child was posed in another way by those involved in the Victoria Espinoza-Campos case. At the age of 21, Espinoza-Campos was shot in the right temple on New Year's Eve. She was pronounced brain dead five days later. But in order to keep her 2½-week-old fetus alive for 10–12 more weeks, doctors attached Espinoza-Campos to breathing machines and a feeding device, something she told relatives she never wanted.

The Journal of the American Medical Association reported in a 1982 article that a brain dead woman who was 23 weeks pregnant, was kept alive artificially for nine weeks until a healthy baby was born. Following the birth, the life support systems were removed and the mother was declared dead. As of 1988 six similar cases had been reported.

Worldwide there is a movement toward transplant surgery from living organs due to shortages of cadaver organs. Charges have been lodged against the Chinese government for removing organs from prisoners against their will for sale to foreign markets. Some fear that such practices will lead to eventual transplant of human brains from "biomorts"—warm bodies with beating hearts that have been pronounced brain dead. Or, as has happened, a fetus is conceived to provide bone marrow for a leukemia victim.

One positive aspect of the brain death standard has been its allowance of organ recovery. With heart-lung death, organs are most often unusable, due to the lack of oxygenated blood provided in a brain death situation. Studies have shown that brain-dead bodies can be sustained for more than six months.

As a society we cannot agree on a definition of when life begins. How then are we to determine when it should end? The legal, moral and ethical questions surrounding death multiply with each uncharted situation that arises. Technological advances present us with quandaries of increasing complexity—all of this as we continue to deny the certainty of our own eventual physical nonexistence.

If there is such a thing as a good or a well death, as the Greeks believed, it can only be defined on an individual basis. Exiting life with control, with courage, with class, with calm, with stoic resignation is what we all imagine and long for. Achieving that goal begins with the question, "What do I, or would I want for my death?" We may certainly increase our prospects of insuring an acceptable outcome through clear communication of what death with dignity means to us personally.

Our knowledge of what it means to die is sorely limited by the fact that we have no experiential basis—we haven't died before. But others have. Through their examples, whatever they might be, and even more importantly through the example of how they lived, we can learn. The real issue, after all, has a lot more to do with life than with death. For it is life that we know and love and desire to maintain. It is life that is therefore so difficult to relinquish. And it is the issues of life—what it means to be alive and living—that we must ultimately determine as we struggle with the question of who should live, who should die, and who should decide.

Chapter Five

Pondering The Realities Of Death

What is life? . . . It departs covertly. . . . Like a thief,
Death took him.
                        —John Gunther, *Death Be Not Proud*

It is a condition of human nature to fear the unknown. As children we fear the dark, unable to see whatever imagined monster or bogeyman might be lurking under the bed, or in the closet, or at the bottom of the stairs. Our fear of death is predicated on the same condition, a fear based on lack of familiarity, understanding and knowledge.

Knowledge is defined as having the ability to recognize and understand something. It means having familiarity with, an association or some experience, or apprehension of the truth. Knowledge means dealing with the facts of a matter and recognizing just what those facts mean.

Based on that definition, why shouldn't we replace our fear of what follows death with knowledge? Why not recognize the facts concerning death? Why not familiarize ourselves with what actually happens so that, armed with the truth, we can allay our fears, overcome our anxieties, and ultimately make an informed personal choice with regard to what we want for ourselves when we die?

As the theologian Paul Tillich wrote in his book *The Courage to Be:*

> *Our anxiety puts frightening masks all over men and things. If we strip them of those masks, their own countenance appears and the fear they produce disappears. This is true even of death. The horrors connected with it are a matter of imagination. They vanish when the mask is taken from the image of death.*[1]

Whatever we imagine the throes of death to be, most often they are not that at all. Having spent 20 years listening to rescue squad workers and emergency room and hospice personnel describe what happens when a person dies, it remained ever so much different in my mind's eye until I was with someone at the moment of death. That someone was my mother.

As often happens preceding death, her lungs had filled with fluid that made her breathing labored and delayed. Her eyes were closed and she was virtually still. There was no sound beyond the so-called "death rattle," that results from fluid being trapped in the throat. She was alive and breathing and then she was not. She had died. She was dead.

It was a moment that I had long dreaded but one that, rather than horrific and terrifying, was rather more intimate and strangely tender than I could have imagined. Just moments before she had spoken my name. It was the last thing she said.

In an episode of the television series *M*A*S*H*, nurse Margaret Houlihan looks up from witnessing the death of a young soldier and asks, "How can someone be alive one minute and dead the next? I'll never understand it." Where does that energy that we know as life go? What happens to the movement, the thought process and the unique, identifiable qualities of the individual persona? How is it that we can go from being what Ernest Becker described as, "a creature with a mind that soars out to speculate about atoms and infinity . . . to being what we also know that we are"— what he calls "worm food"?[2]

Over a century ago, as he was assisting with the autopsy of the slain President Abraham Lincoln, Dr. Edward Curtis asked much the same thing. Where does that energy we know as life go and how can it be transformed so quickly into what we call death?

Dr. Woodward and I proceeded to open the head and remove the brain down to the track of the ball . . . when as I was lifting that latter from the cavity of the skull, suddenly the bullet dropped out through my fingers and fell, breaking the solemn silence of the room with its clatter into an empty basin that was standing beneath. There it lay upon the white china, a little black mass no bigger than the end of my finger—dull and motionless and harmless, yet the cause of such mighty changes in the world's history as we may perhaps never realize. . . . Silently, in one corner of the room, I prepared the brain for weighing. As I looked at the soft gray and white substance that I was carefully washing, it was impossible to realize that it was merely clay upon whose workings but the day before, rested the hopes of the nation. I felt more profoundly impressed than ever with the mystery of that unknown something which may be named "vital spark" as well as anything else, whose absence or presence makes all the immeasurable difference between an inert mass of matter owing obedience to no laws but those governing the physical and chemical forces of the universe, and on the other hand, a living brain by whose silent, subtle machinery a world may be ruled . . .[3]

The philosophical aspects of death require individual reflection and conclusion. The physical aspects remain universally the same. They begin with impending signs of death that include a drop in body temperature and a slowing down of the circulatory system which may result in the lips turning bluish and forming into mottled spots under the skin. Those spots are called petechiae and they are used by medical examiners as one determination of the time of death. As death nears, the senses no longer function properly. Hearing is the last sense lost. Urinary and bowel muscles expel any waste left in the body. And then it is over.

Some hospitals, such as New York's Memorial Sloan-Kettering, allow the family up to an hour in which to say a personal goodbye to the deceased before the body is removed. In most hospitals and nursing homes, families are discouraged from seeing the corpse. It is dispensed to the morgue or funeral home as hastily as possible. Gurneys used to transport the body are camouflaged so that persons passing one in a hospital or nursing home hallway are not aware of the contents.

Immediately following death, the request for an autopsy or orders for one may be made. Hospitals and nursing homes once relied upon autopsy reports to prove that they were not negligent in matters of providing proper care. Some no longer do so. The medical examiner (or coroner, if it is an elected rather than an appointed position), may order an autopsy if there is some question as to cause of death. The death of an infant or an adolescent, for no apparent reason, often warrants the ordering of such autopsies. Children's deaths are carefully investigated to determine if there is possible child abuse involved. Should the medical examiner or coroner order an autopsy, the family may not override his or her ruling without going to court.

The autopsy, also known as a post-mortem, is performed by a pathologist under the guidance of the medical examiner or coroner. Autopsies normally take from one to four hours. The purpose of an autopsy is to determine cause of death as well as the approximate time that death occurred. This is done through surgical examination of the body.

When my college roommate (the one I had discussed issues of death and dying with during our school years) was kidnapped and murdered, her body was not found for over a week. The body was then held almost another week for investigative and autopsy purposes. When the body was finally released to the funeral home, I was asked to go there to view her remains. I did so in order to let her mother know whether or not I felt an open casket would be appropriate.

At that time I had never seen a corpse, nor did I know what I now do about autopsy and embalming procedures. Later, as I listened over and over again to the medical examiner describe autopsies, I would think of the day I saw my friend lying in her casket. Like many of the autopsies the medical examiner described for my students, my roommate's autopsy had been done to help solve a murder.

There are five ways, and only five, that we can die. They are homicide (murder), suicide, accident, disease, or from natural causes. It is standard procedure that an autopsy be performed on any victim of a suspected crime. It also is standard procedure to conduct an autopsy on the body of anyone executed for a crime, such as murder.

If we die in a hospital or a nursing home, as approximately 80 percent of us will, the cause of death is often evident and thus can be recorded on the death certificate without further investigation. Homicides and suicides are not always as transparent. Because the cause of death has

such important ramifications for legal and insurance purposes, medical examiners must be as accurate as possible
in determining how a person died, or what was the cause
of death.

When called to a death scene, the medical examiner
waits until every aspect of the area has been photographed. Nothing may be touched or moved or added to
the scene unnecessarily. If there is a rope around the victim's neck or a knife in his stomach, it is left there.

*In death, Brian was not a pretty sight. No one knew for sure
how long his body had lain in an abandoned south side building before a scavenger discovered it. Now, two days later, his
body rested on a cold steel gurney in the morgue examining
room, reserved for decomposed victims, his wrists, ankles, and
mouth still bound with duct tape. A small hole in the middle
of the forehead of this twenty-one-year-old man appeared to be
a fatal gunshot wound.* [4]

When a homicide victim is found, his hands are
"gloved" in brown paper bags to protect evidence under
the fingernails or on the hands. Brown paper bags keep the
blood from molding, should there be blood present. The
victim's body is placed inside a zippered body bag or
pouch that is used one time only. It is then removed to the
morgue, laid out on a table and photographed both
clothed and unclothed once again in detail. The body bag
and the victim's clothing are saved. Each may contain evi-
dentiary fibers, hairs, skin particles, fluids, blood, or other
things relevant to determining the cause of death.

The basic autopsy procedure involves opening up
the body from the neck and shoulder area to the groin. This
is done by making a Y-shaped incision that allows removal
of the breastbone as well as vital organs and the intestines.
Examination of the intestines reveals when and what the
deceased last ate. That may help in establishing time of

death as well as where the person was when he or she died.

As the organs are removed from the body, each is weighed and carefully examined. Tissue slices of each are taken for chemical testing. In most cases, the organs are returned with the cadaver to the funeral home for embalming. The organs are disinfected with a solution such as Paulex and then placed back inside the body cavity before it is sewn shut.

In order to reach the brain for post-mortem examination, the skull cap is removed. This involves making an incision from ear to ear, across the top of the head. Most women have enough hair to cover over the incision, but for some men who are balding it may be necessary to later hide the incision with a casket pillow. The skills of the funeral director who embalms and cosmetizes the body make it unlikely to detect signs of autopsy at a visitation or viewing.

Autopsies may reveal all sorts of information about the causes and circumstances surrounding a death. Some examples include:

1. Darkish blue splotches, called lividity, form in areas where there is no direct contact or pressure on the body, whereas whitish blanched-out areas might be left by close contact or pressure. This may indicate the position of the body at the time of death.
2. Blood splatters and drops help identify what type of weapon was used, at what range, and at what strength. They may also indicate where the body was at the time of death and what kind of blow occurred.
3. Maggots removed from the corpse can be timed on how long it takes them to replicate—the number of generations on the corpse may indicate how long the deceased has been dead.

4. Fluid drawn from an eyeball by syringe may reveal drug usage that is not otherwise detectable.

In today's violent society, medical examiners are overwhelmed with work. Determining the identity of a homicide victim can take a long time. Sometimes murderers try to remove the victim's identity by knocking out teeth or cutting off fingers. The victim's body may be set ablaze, dismembered or doused with acid to further hinder positive identification.

Of the 4,500 autopsies conducted in Chicago's Cook County in 1991, almost 1,000 were homicides. Los Angeles County reported a 9-to-15-day delay in performing autopsies, due to overwork. And the emotional toll on those involved is almost without measure.

Dr. Jones remembered being particularly bothered by the case of a 6-year-old who had been abducted while playing in the street, brutalized and dumped in a garbage can for the mother to find. "Trying to separate your outrage from being just a scientist is very difficult to do, especially when you're dealing with children," Jones said. "There's a tremendous emotional toll that I don't think you can appreciate."

"You never really get used to it," said Robert Nicks, an assistant in the autopsy room for 15 years and himself a grandfather. He described his first week on the job as full of "bad dreams, little sleep, and a lot of drinking."[5]

As part of their post-mortem work, medical examiners are expected to determine, as nearly as possible, an approximate time of death. This is invaluable in solving murder cases. The presence of maggots on the corpse and how recently the deceased had last eaten are two clues. Algor mortis, or cooling of the body, is another indicator. The human body cools at a rate of about 1½ degrees per hour under normal (that is, nonfreezing or excessively hot) conditions. A deep-core temperature may be taken from the corpse by use of a rectal thermometer.

Rigor mortis, or stiffening of the body due to formation of lactic acids, is also used to determine time of death. Approximately 12 hours after death the corpse will have reached its stiffest point, with the fingers and the jaw stiffening first. Between the 13th and 24th hours after death, the corpse goes flaccid again. Livor mortis, which is how fast the blood settles out to dependent parts of the body, can also aid the medical examiner in deciding at about what time a person died.

Despite all his or her training and all the advancements in the areas of forensics and pathology, sometimes the medical examiners still cannot know for certain how a person died. Nor can the time of death always be pinpointed. One 12-year-old girl who died in a big city hospital of possible pneumonia had two months earlier tried to hang herself. During her first hospitalization from the suicide attempt, cocaine and Valium were found in her blood. Based on such circumstances, it was impossible to make a final determination as to how she died.

Questions may also linger when death is caused by accident. We as a society ascribe to the "whole body concept," which assumes an entire, identifiable corpse will remain when death occurs. But recent bombings and airplane crashes have proven otherwise. A powerful enough blast will literally vaporize bodies.

The bomb blast in Lebanon that killed over 200 U.S. Marines was so powerful that shreds of servicemen's shorts were found embedded in concrete walls left standing by the explosion. When a commuter plane crashed in the Midwest, some 1,200 body parts from 68 people were all that was found. The largest weighed about four pounds.

What we do in order to identify and reassemble bodies, as well as why we do it, raises many questions. Whatever the answers, the body itself, regardless of how it came to die, holds tremendous significance as the last vestige of our selfhood.

Perhaps that is why the process of embalming the body, unlike an autopsy of it, is seldom questioned. In addition to the psychological aspects, embalming or preserving of the corpse has two other major benefits. One is sanitation. Cocci, or disease-causing organisms, cover a decomposing body. When a corpse reaches the embalming room, it is immediately placed on a stainless steel or porcelain table and disinfected. A soapy germicidal solution containing bleach is used, with special attention given to the nose and mouth areas. Hepatitis-B and AIDS victims undergo special measures during the embalming process to insure that the individual doing the embalming is amply protected from possible contamination.

We are one of the few cultures in the world that embalms our dead. Borrowed from the ancient Egyptians, the practice of embalming was not widely used in the United States until the Civil War when it made possible the sending home of bodies of soldiers killed on distant battlefields. During the 1800's and early 1900's, embalming was usually done in the home of the deceased, most often in the kitchen. The body of Jacqueline Kennedy-Onassis was rumored to have been embalmed in her 5th Avenue apartment, following her death there in 1994.

Embalming is not required by law except in cases where the body is to be transported some distance. As previously mentioned, embalming does aid greatly in the sanitation process. It is more commonly thought of, however, as preserving the body for viewing. An unembalmed body quickly discolors, bloats and putrefies. With the embalming process, a body may be preserved for some time.

The actual embalming process involves removal of blood and its replacement with a formaldehyde solution that will preserve the tissue. Before beginning the procedure, the body is positioned on the embalming table with legs extended and arms at the sides. The genital area is covered with a piece of cloth. The chest cavity is elevated above the abdomen and the head above the chest by placing it on a rubber block. This prevents gravitation of blood from the heart to the head, which might cause discoloration.

Any rigor mortis is relieved by massaging the body's extremities, after which fingers may be glued together. The nose is tilted slightly to the right for a more natural look as people gaze at the corpse in the casket. It may be straightened with cotton wadding, which is also used in the mouth to prevent leakage.

Embalming takes place through the arterial system. The usual points of injection are the carotid artery (passing up the neck to the head) and the femoral artery (chief artery of the thigh). An incision is made below the neck along the collarbone to expose the carotid artery, which is lifted with aneurysm hooks and tied off. The artery is incised about four milimeters. If blood clots are present, they are removed with forceps.

A cannula inserted into the carotid artery carries embalming fluid into the body's vascular system from a pressurized embalming machine. The embalming fluid is mixed with water and flows through a rubber hose to the cannula inserted into the artery.

White splotching on the body indicates effective embalming. Areas such as the toes and feet, fingers and hands, thorax and face may require individuallyadministered injections of embalming fluid. If the pressure of injection fluids is too high, blisters may appear. Improper mixtures of embalming chemicals, sometimes in tandem with chemicals already present in the body, can cause the corpse to turn green or yellow or occasionally even to twitch. Colorants are sometimes added to the embalming fluid to prevent discoloration problems or to overcome the yellow effect brought on by hepatitis or the reddish flush caused by asphyxiation involving carbon monoxide.

While the embalming fluid is entering on one side, blood is being forced out by embalming fluid on the other side. A second incision, below the neck along the collarbone, allows for insertion of a rubber tube to carry the blood. It drains down the side of the embalming table, which is lipped and slightly tilted. At the present time, blood removed through the embalming process often goes directly into the sewer system.

Another procedure done to help preserve the body involves the use of an instrument called a trocar. It is a sharply pointed shaft that is inserted into the abdominal region for removal of fecal and other waste materials lodged there.

To insure that the viewing of the body eliminates as much distaste as possible, extensive cosmetizing is performed on the corpse. Any extraneous facial hair—in the eye area, in the nose, or on the face itself—is plucked or trimmed. The eyelids are lifted and plastic caps (large contact lens-looking objects with prongs) are placed over the eyeballs to hold the eyelids shut. Marbles or cotton balls are sometimes used to replace missing eyeballs.

The jaw is clamped shut by injection of metal wires into the gums, which are then tied off. The mouth is carefully shut and sometimes the gums are glued to ensure a natural, pleasant expression.

Collagen may be injected into the nose, cheeks, chin or lips to fill and plump them. If parts of the head, face or upper body have been disfigured or destroyed, clay or wax replacements may be constructed. Autopsied bodies may require more attention to insure that incisions, such as ones across the skull, are adequately covered.

Funeral homes will request that the family provide cosmetics that were normally used by the deceased, sometimes including cologne or perfume. Beyond that, the person doing the cosmetizing may use wax, gloss, powder, skin tint or whatever is felt to be necessary to achieve a more lifelike appearance.

A professional hairdresser is usually called in to style women's hair. Often a photograph of the deceased is used to determine the proper hair and cosmetic styling. Nails are manicured and painted, sometimes to cover up discoloration. With that, the body is lifted onto a dressing table by means of a hoist and dressed according to the family's wishes.

Complete dressing includes undergarments and shoes, if they can be fitted on. Embalmed bodies swell slightly so clothing may need adjustment. Only when absolutely necessary is clothing cut down the back or heavily pinned.

Once the corpse is fully dressed, it is then placed in the casket. What follows is up to the individual wishes of the family. Before the casket is locked and sealed, it is possible to have such items as jewelry and eyeglasses removed from the body.

Personal objects and mementos may also be placed in the casket, alongside the body, for burial and cremation. A student from our high school, who died of a congenital illness, was laid to rest surrounded by letters written by his classmates and friends as expressions of their caring for him. One of my acquaintences was buried with his favorite walking stick and a certificate from McDonald's from one of his grandchildren.

Much of this information on the autopsy and embalming processes that may follow death is not at all what we imagined. Possibly, it is also something we would prefer not to know. And why? Because in our death-denying society, that once natural and intimate interplay between living and dying has been systematically and deliberately eliminated, leaving us to approach the dead as strangers, summarily distanced from us through their mysterious and repellent condition that we choose to keep unknowable. No longer do we gather around the deathbed in hopes of gleaning some understanding of death's unfolding transformation. Nor do we listen for that revelation from the dying that might make us less afraid to die in turn. Neither do we care for the dead, as we once did for them when they were still living.

Instead we leave it to others to handle the aftermath of death until all is tidy and sanitized once again. Strangers determine when and how death occurs. Strangers handle what follows death. Someone else bathes and clothes and caskets our loved ones, while we await reunion with a sanitized, cosmetized corpse that only further distances us from the actuality of what has occurred.

During the 20-some years that I taught a course on death and dying, I observed some 2,000 students absorbing information on autopsy and embalming as they listened to the medical examiner and visited the funeral home. The most telling moment came as they approached the embalming room. Some of the so-called toughest among them turned away. Others entered to stare their own personal mortality in the face.

Our follow-up discussions on what they had heard and seen never resulted in consensus on whether or not to autopsy and/or embalm. There was, however, general agreement that it was better to know than to imagine. And most importantly for them, the experiencing of such sober realities focused their attention where it belonged—on living. Their knowledge, understanding and familiarity with issues of death made them aware of the fragility and finitude of their individual beings. No longer as frightened by death, they became instead grateful for simply being alive.

What the dead represent, for each of us, is the certitude that we too shall die, be dead, become a corpse or parts thereof—that it is only a breath or a heartbeat that separates them from us. If we were only willing to unmask and thus demystify the image of death, perhaps then we, too, might be able to stare our own human mortality in the face. In so doing, we might free ourselves from that gnawing dread and unacknowledged anxiety that so distorts the focus of our daily lives, and in the process discover that same gratitude, based on knowledge, insight and understanding.

Chapter Six

Cultural And Historic Viewpoints On What Follows Death

I've heard the songs from tombs of old, that praise life on earth and belittle the land of the dead. Why is this done to the Land of Eternity? It has no terrors.
                                        —from *A Harper's Song*

As much as we may fear facing death, we also wonder what follows. What really happens when we die? Where, if anywhere, do we go? What, if anything, becomes of us? Throughout history people and cultures have illuminated their visions of life most clearly through the answers offered in response to such questions.

Whatever the answers may be, each response reflects thought and caring as well as an attempt to comfort both the dying and those left behind by their death. Mythology, religious teachings, literature, art and music embody such efforts. So, too, do death customs and rituals stemming from the beliefs about death adhered to by varied cultures.

Since much of that which we believe and practice has been borrowed and adapted over time, understanding the death customs of those from whom we have adapted and borrowed may offer more insight into personal feelings about human mortality than might be imagined. Why, for instance, is the practice of embalming frowned upon in the Jewish and Muslim sectors while heavily sanctioned in our own Judeo-Christian society? Why do Hindus and Buddhists embrace death as a liberator while we tend to view it as an oppressor, the feared and dreaded enemy? How have other societies responded to aging and terminal illness, suicide and euthanasia? Is there anything we can learn through consideration of their viewpoints? And what of grief? Are there approaches and outlooks, customs and rituals that offer more comfort to the bereaved than those we tend to follow unquestioningly?

While most of us remain largely ignorant of the history attached to our own death practices and perspectives, we remain fascinated by those of the ancient Egyptians. What is it that so intrigues us? What holds us so timelessly spellbound? Why the desire to know every detail of their post-mortem rituals and the philosophy that created them?

No segment of human history captivates the imagination in the way Egyptian history does. That may be in part related to a need to reconnect with death in a way that the Egyptians seemed to be doing. It is a recognition that, beginning with earliest man, life and death were inextricably woven in such a way as to add meaning to human existence that we seem to have lost. Perhaps we envy their ability to accept death in a way that our own death-denying culture cannot, but should.

My most vivid memory of Egypt was standing over the partially unwrapped remains of Pharaoh Rameses II in the Mummy Room at the Cairo Museum. I wondered then how his subjects would have felt about his being there, on display. It struck me that, as part of the Egyptian entombment ritual, Rameses' mummy would have passed through a "room of handing over," signifying his passage from the world of the living to the preferred and protected world of the dead. Now he was back from that passage, enclosed in a glass-topped coffin with remnants of teeth, hair and flesh all discernible.

Rameses lived well into his 90's. He not only ruled over Egypt longer than any other pharaoh, he might have left more progeny as well. By some accounts he fathered over 100 children. A gravesite believed to hold the remains of some of those offspring was recently found.

The man who would rule Egypt some 2,000 years after Rameses, Anwar Sadat, decreed that the exhibition of mummies be discontinued. Recently, however, the Mummy Room at the Cairo Museum has been reopened.

The recent discovery of a 2,000-year-old cemetery at an oasis 230 miles southwest of Cairo was heralded as an event equal to the discovery of King Tut's tomb in 1922. While archaeologists delighted in the prospect of learning even more about Egyptian death rituals through access to these pristine remains, wholly unscathed by looters, some raised the issue of just how appropriate the disturbance of such a burial site is. How would we feel about someone digging up corpses in our cemeteries in order to learn about our past? Isn't that grave robbing, and under current law considered a crime?

Whatever our philosophical viewpoint on the propriety of digging up human remains, it is hard to ignore what can be learned from them about ancient death customs. It is equally difficult to quell the curiosity they inspire. Consciously or not, we all seek answers to the seemingly impenetrable and often disconcerting questions posed by death. Can a better understanding of the rituals

surrounding the dead—what we do for and with them—
help us in formulating answers to our questions? Perhaps
they can.

We know from the placement of remains in prehistoric burial sites that even early man had concern for the
dead. Bodies were often laid on their sides in a fetal position. Red ocher was smeared on the body to simulate
blood, the source of life. Herbs and flowers were scattered
over the corpse. Some, such as marigold and bee balm,
were perceived to have healing qualities, others were used
to cover the smell of decay.

Tools and other personal possessions were often
buried with the corpse. Sometimes the objects left in the
grave were "killed," broken deliberately so that no one else
could use them. This may have been an attempt to prevent
the dead from contaminating the living or to keep them
from returning to life.

The corpse itself might have stab wounds from animal horns or cuts in the skull to assure its non-return. The
use of gravestones or slabs most likely originated from that
same prehistoric concern for keeping the dead weighted
down.

Though we will probably never know for certain
why, most corpses were fully dressed and then wrapped in
animal skins with the fur facing inside. Many bodies were
tattooed, some had shaved heads and eyebrows.
Sometimes corpses were buried together, as with a mother
and child. The mother's legs were deliberately pulled up
so that the child's body could rest at her feet. All this
would seem to indicate concern for the dead and what was
to become of them.

Further evidence that our early ancestors associated
death with spiritual concerns has been found in an ancient
Israeli cave site. A man buried there held in his hand an

antler—perhaps an ancient precursor, to the tomb offerings of King Tut.

Like each human being who has followed him, early man was perplexed by the occurrence and the outcome of death. Something prompted prehistoric peoples some 16,000 years ago to lower themselves into the bowels of the earth and there create artwork on the walls of caves. Why not above ground? And why the recurrence of cave paintings in far-flung areas of the world—Africa and Asia, North America and Europe—at a time when the inhabitants of each continent had not the slightest inkling that their counterparts thousands of miles away were following the same ritualistic pursuit?

To better understand the role of cave paintings in early death rituals, I applied to the French Ministry of Culture for admission to the Caves of Lascaux. Described as the Sistine Chapel of ancient history, access to these French caves is limited to five visitors per month in order to prevent further deterioration of the paintings caused by high levels of carbon dioxide. A replica of the caves has been created nearby to accommodate others. In our group of five were two archaeologists, an anthropologist, myself, and a Frenchman whose life work was studying cave art in China.

Clearly our respective reasons for seeking access to the caves differed but it was with one incredulous gasp of awe and wonderment that we reacted to what had so deliberately been created to sanctify their walls. Along them and above us on the ceiling appeared the undulating bodies of horses and bulls, carefully contoured to the shape and form of the rock canvas on which they were painted. Their primal gaze met ours, their eyes followed us, they were alive and animated and infused with motion. Among them there was but a single human figure, a stick-man with the head of a bird, lying dead as they coursed about him. The significance of that inert figure is something we may never know for certain.

It is known that early man sometimes used birds as a symbol of death, which might explain the figure's bird head. Further, we know that early humans believed in the animistic ability of inanimate objects to come to life. Were these cave paintings used as part of a ritual to protect the living? Was this an attempt to ward off death? Was there acknowledgement in the painting that death was an inevitable outcome or rather some statement about what followed it? Early man's beliefs about death and afterlife are largely speculative.

Whatever their meaning, the artistic sensitivity and timeless beauty of the cave paintings at Lascaux are alluring reminders of the common bonds that unify all human existence. The universal desire to establish a meaning to that existence and to leave behind some tangible reminder of it is a common longing. Seventeen thousand years ago, or today, what we seek is the same.

So we turn again to the Egyptians, a group who left clear and tangible evidence of their perspective on life and death. Death, to them, was simply a joyous extension of life, a chance to do it all, in glorious repetition, again and again for eternity. Whether at Giza or in the Valley of the Kings, near Thebes, "houses for eternity" (tombs, pyramids, and temples) were constructed shortly after the birth of pharaohs to insure them a lasting place in which to pursue such pleasures. Some 2-1/2 million blocks of stone, many weighing up to two tons each, were fashioned into pyramids that soared as high as 481 feet. Inside the tombs, the walls were adorned with paintings, which pictured the pleasures and glories of one's past life.

Special spaces were designated for the mummy-wrapped corpse, the body organs stored in canopic jars and the personal possessions of the deceased. False passageways and doors opening to nothing were designed to deter grave robbers that would be heard by spirits as they stepped on brittle mummy beads scattered throughout the crypt.[1]

Statues with hollow eyes watched over the tomb's interior. Looking out from a statue representing the deceased was Ba, a human-headed bird who guarded the tomb. Ba could leave the tomb at night in order to bring back information from the world of the living. Having entered the body at birth, with the first breath of life, and departed at the moment of death, Ba represented the dead's character or personality.

Food and wine, toiletries, jewelry and clothing, furniture and games, animistic statues of servants and pets, sometimes even mummified animals, were placed in the tombs for use by the ka, the dead person's spiritual copy or soul. The ka, the Egyptians believed, continued living in the afterworld, repeating all the best and favorite life experiences of the deceased.

Some five thousand gold items, including his throne, were entombed with the remains of King Tutankhamun (Tut). Because he favored duck, hundreds were smoked for his post-mortem dining pleasure. Wine and beer, both favorite Egyptian beverages, were also placed in his tomb.

In order that his spirit might follow the sun across the blue ocean of the sky, three boats were provided for the Pharaoh Khufu known to the Greeks as Cheops. Two were for promenading the heavens and one for visiting the holy city of Heliopolis. To protect the Pharaoh, the oars were embossed with arrows, "so that the spirit sailor could attack any enemies."

Just as the sun crossed the sky in a real gold boat, so did its children, the pharaohs. Daily the sun appeared and disappeared but never vanished or died. Following it to their cemeteries, west of the Nile, insured the pharaohs resurrection as their souls conquered space.

Preparation of the corpse for the afterlife was a lengthy and varied procedure. First the body was taken to Ibu, the tent of purification, where priests cleansed it to symbolize rebirth. Next the brain was removed, sometimes through a small hole in the ethmoid bone at the top of the nostril or other times, as the Greek historian, Herodotus described, by the use of iron hooks to pull parts of the brain through the nostrils. Another method used was the making of an incision at the nape of the neck for access to the skull. Following removal of the brain, a thin coating of resin was applied to the face.

The body was next taken to Wabet, the place of embalming, where a long incision was made with a flint knife to the left side of the abdomen. The incision allowed for removal of the lungs, stomach, intestines and liver, but not the heart. The heart was believed by Egyptians to be the seat of wisdom and must remain with the body, to be weighed by the Jackal, Anubis. Should Anubis find the heart as light as a feather (free of guilt and remorse), the dead would be admitted to paradise. But should the heart weigh heavily against the feather on the other side of Anubis' scales, the Pig Destroyer—Devourer of Millions of Years—awaited in the underworld.

Desecrating the body of the dead by removal of organs contradicted the Egyptian belief that the body should be intact and as nearly perfect as possible for the eternal life ahead. But they also understood that the body could not be effectively preserved were it left full of rotting entrails, so they placed the organs in canopic jars next to the mummified corpse, rationalizing that some restoration would occur after death. Their concern for the body's condition led them to make artificial limbs and body parts (even breasts) to replace those lost to surgery, accident or mutilation. The priest who had cut open the body for organ removal was symbolically stoned by his fellow-priests to assuage his act of desecration.

For 40 days the corpse was then packed in a solution of natron, (a natural salt of sodium carbonate, sodium bicarbonate, sodium sulfate and sodium chloride), which preserved the body by removing moisture and thus retarding decay. Next, the corpse was sent to the house of beauty, called Per Nefer.

At Per Nefer the body was carefully washed, sometimes with palm wine. The body cavity was stuffed with resin-soaked linen, as well as fragrances such as myrrh and cassia, lichens, onions, mud, sawdust, more natron and sometimes a papyrus scroll with information about the life of the deceased. The incision made by the priest to remove organs was then sewn up and sealed with wax or covered with a metal plate. Body orifices were plugged with linen and the skin was rubbed with juniper oil, beeswax, spices, milk, and wine.

Cosmetic procedures included padding of the eyes and cheeks (the eyes were usually left in place, though sometimes flattened). Later, artificial eyes were used. A gold "tongue" was placed between the lips to restore speech to the dead. Women's breasts were padded and the nipples coated with gold leaf. Faces were rouged, men with red ocher and women with yellow, the eyes of both highlighted, and henna applied to the hands and feet. Special jewelry was designed and used for ornamenting the cosmetized corpse.[2]

Finally the corpse was wrapped in layers of linen bandages which were anywhere from two to eight inches wide. Originally natural in color, the bandages were later dyed red, blue or yellow. They were woven especially for the dead by professional weavers.

Wrapping the corpse in bandages was a ritual in itself. Step by step, the corpse was swathed, making sure that in the process the head and shoulders stayed affixed to the neck and that the arms and legs were secured closely to the body. Even the male genitals were specially wrapped for protection inside the mummy.

Our word mummy was taken from the Persian word for bitumen which is moumia and means coal. It may have referred to the darkening process that took place on the remains and bandages of mummified corpses. The linen bandages were interspersed with tree resin, which often turned black and glassy. Other materials applied to the bandages included honey and myrrh. Depending on the amounts applied, the mummy would darken a little or a lot.

Among the linen bandages were tucked jewels and amulets to ward off evils spirits, a favorite being the scarab (beetle). Over all of this, a shroud was wrapped. Then the mummy was adorned with gold and more jewelry as well as a mask that covered the face and shoulders. The most dazzling example of such a mask was that of the young King Tut. His mask was a likeness of his boyish face reflecting his premature death at the age of 18 or 19.

Carefully, the mummy was then ensconced in several caskets, which fit one into the other. The outer coffin was carved in the likeness of the corpse it held with hands folded over the chest and feet drawn together.

On the 70th day after death, mourners assembled at the home of the dead. A procession which included servants carrying possessions, canopic jars, ushabti (figures of clay to perform the wishes of the deceased in the tomb), a statue of the dead, as well as his or her coffin, proceeded to the site of entombment. There priests clad in leopard skins ritualistically touched the mummy's mouth with an adze to restore its senses. The spirit, ka, was released by the cutting of bandages around the lips of a "mummified" priest who simulated the dead person.

After appropriate offerings, including the leg of an ox to restore sexual powers, there followed incantations. The tools used to embalm were placed near the deceased before the tomb was sealed with the seal of the necropolis. Following a funeral feast, bare-breasted wives (if a husband died), and other mourners smeared themselves with dirt as a sign of respect for the departed.

Yearly celebrations and offerings continued in the belief that the living must speak the name of the dead in order to guarantee immortality—the true essence of one's individuality was felt to be one's name. In the beginning it was held that only the pharaoh could ascend to eternity, but later the possibility was held out for all, even the poor, whose organs rotted and liquefied, having simply been soaked in natron in an attempt to save the body as best they could. For the poor, mummification usually involved injections of oil of cedar through the anus, then plugging the orifice until the oil dissolved the internal organs. Their pyramid, or house for eternity, was a simple grave in the desert.

Egyptians of every ilk longed for transformation into Akh, a mummy transported through the winding roads to enter the Region of the Happy Ones, there to dwell blissfully forever. Based upon such a philosophy of life and death, the ancient Egyptians spent their lives preparing to die, and anticipating with great relish what would follow death. What an extraordinary approach to death, to spend your life preparing for it in fearless anticipation.

Unlike their Egyptian neighbors, the life and freedom-loving Greeks did not embrace death with such zeal. Instead they worshipped youth and abhorred the thought of growing old. This life was what the Greeks adored.

Once the ability to see light, and thereby beauty, was taken from their eyes, there remained for the Greeks only gloomy darkness. An eternity spent in darkness was not to be coveted.

The transitions between light and darkness (life and death), was the responsibility of Thanatos, God of Death, and his twin brother, Hypnos, God of Sleep. According to Greek mythology, the brothers would appear to mortals, signaling their demise. Cutting a lock of hair in preparation for Hades, the sons of Nyx (goddess of the Night), would then carry the deceased away to the River Styx where the boatman, Charon, awaited to ferry them across to the underworld.

The Greeks believed that death separated the soul from the body. Ever after, the soul dwelt as a "shade" in Hades. According to the Greek poet, Homer, only those spirits guilty of extreme sin were punished in Hades. The rest merely prowled about eternally in the dark. The reward of eternal happiness on the Blessed Isles or the Elysian Fields was reserved for only a very few Greek heroes.

Ancient Greek funeral practices were markedly similar to our own. The corpse was bathed, perfumed, and then dressed in the best garments available. For three days the corpse lay surrounded by flowers, until accompanied by mourners clad in black, the pottery or wooden coffin was taken to its place of disposal. There a funeral oration was delivered. Since it was believed by the Greeks that the soul of the departed was still present, nothing but good was spoken.

Before leaving the tomb, wreathes of flowers were placed upon it. Flowers served a dual purpose at Greek funerals. They symbolized victory over death while simultaneously masking unpleasant odors possibly emanating from the corpse. Myrtle was a commonly used flower.

Strangely, so was celery. Before returning home to attend a funeral feast, the Greeks would place a gold coin under the tongue of the dead. That coin, they believed, would serve as payment to the boatman Charon for transporting the dead across the River Styx to Hades.

The ancient Greeks used both burial and cremation as methods of body disposal. Graves were often adorned with simple architectural details such as columns, slabs, draped urns, or a single pillar. That aspect of our own funerary art was likely borrowed from them. Vases given to young Greek women by their mothers as wedding gifts were placed on the graves of girls who did not marry. It was required that survivors visit the grave of the dead on the third, ninth, and thirtieth day after death had occurred. The childless adopted heirs to insure such visits. Depictions of grave scenes on Greek vases show more women than men engaged in these ritual visits.

In parts of modern-day Greece it is customary to bury a body only until such time as the remains are reduced to a skeletal form. Subsequently, the bones are disinterred and placed in an ossuary (storage area for human bones), in order to vacate the burial space for other corpses.

One of my Greek-American students described attending a ceremony for the transferal of his grandfather's remains from grave to ossuary. He noted how lovingly his family members held and touched the bones of his grandfather, and how natural the process seemed for them. What he had expected to suffer through, he instead found to be an experience of intimacy between the living and the dead. That, he said, gave him comfort and a lasting bond with his grandfather, both in life and in death.

In the Eastern world of Buddhism, death at any age is seen as a means of moving closer to nirvana, where reincarnations cease and the soul becomes at rest in the universe. Buddhists believe, as did the ancient Greeks, that ghosts may return from there to haunt the family. Caught between reincarnations because of negative thoughts occurring at the time of death, ghosts can only achieve rebirth through the offerings of their living kin. It is for these ghosts, as well as for all of one's dead ancestors, that flowers, food, incense and wooden prayer sticks or paper prayers are offered to insure passage to the next life.

The Burmese call such ghosts, trapped between reincarnations, "Pe." During a visit to Burma, my husband and I were invited to the home of a devout Buddhist family for dinner. As the meal progressed, we kept hearing a scratching sound that seemed to be coming from the roof, directly over the table where we were seated. Eventually the host and hostess acknowledged the scratching sound, explaining that it was a Pe, (a ghost), that had not yet been released to the next reincarnation. They did not say whose ghost it was.

To properly prepare for that transition, devout Buddhists, such as the Burmese, dress their dead in odd-numbered layers of clothing and then watch over the dead for an odd number of days before cremation takes place. Odd numbers are considered to be fortuitous. Oftentimes a valuable gem (equivalent to the Greek or Roman use of a coin), is placed inside the corpse's mouth for use as barter in the afterworld. Money may also be burned at the funeral service, as an offering to accompany the dead to their next reincarnation.

Devout Buddhists in Vietnam attempted to keep the spirits of MIA skeletons satisfied by supplying them with food and drink. If available, Western food such as hamburgers or hot dogs were placed before the skeleton. Eventually the three daily meals were reduced to one and after three months discontinued altogether. Cultural interpretations of death such as this reflect how differently death is viewed by various peoples. When Buddhist monks in Vietnam set themselves ablaze in protest of the war, Western observers were shocked and horrified. To Vietnamese Buddhists, however, their act simply represented release into a more desirable state of being.

In the Himalayan country of Tibet, Buddhists practice something called "sky burial." The two-hour ritual is usually performed at dawn. Cost for the service ranges from $7–$40, depending on what the family can afford to pay. In this frigid area above the timberline, where wood is at a premium, total cremation of a body would not be practical. Consequently, they have adopted an alternative. The alternative consists of removing flesh from the corpse, then pulverizing the bones, which are then mixed with barley meal. The mixture is fed to the vultures, followed by the flesh, which is cut into small pieces. This follows the Buddhist precept that even a dead body may be of use to a fellow creature.

Both China and Japan were traditionally considered to be Buddhist countries, but China was also heavily influenced by the teachings of Confucius, who, unlike the Buddhists, prescribed burial over cremation. It was the Chinese Communists who reintroduced the ancient but abandoned practice of cremation, begun as early as the Qin Dynasty (221–207 BC). Their reasons for doing so were twofold. One was to dispel feudal ideas and superstitions surrounding burial. The other was to save timber, being used in large quantities for caskets.

For some time the Communist government was successful in promoting cremation among its people. The party's own leaders, such as Premier Zhou Enlai, set an example by ordering their remains cremated, following death. Chairman Mao, who had originally signed the cremation edict in the early 1950's, would not have wanted his body preserved in a memorial hall, as it still is, but rather cremated, said his successor, Deng Xiaoping, who along with Mao signed the edict. Despite such expressions by the Communist leadership, however, only about 30 percent of China's approximately six million deaths per year are followed by cremation. For the other 70 percent of China's people, who are predominately inhabitants of rural areas, Taoist, Buddhist and Confucian practices continue to outweigh the wishes of the government. This group continues to prefer burial of the dead, of utmost importance in ancient China, following decrees by the Ming and Qing emperors forbidding cremation.

Confucianism taught that one's body comes from the parents and should therefore not be destroyed. A true sign of respect toward one's parents was the purchase of a good coffin, selected for them while they were still alive and well. Thickness of such coffins indicated status and position among the Chinese.

One of the most poignent sites I witnessed during a visit to China was a grave alongside a river in the rural countryside. It was marked with straw tied together to form a protective umbrella-like covering over a mound of dirt. Also atop the mound was a strip of white cloth attached to a pole. Not far away stood a brick crematory.

Recently, a village family from the Hubei Province chose to follow the teachings of Confucius when their only son died. After 10 hours of unconsciousness, the teenager was surreptitiously buried. His death was not reported so as to avoid the government-required cremation.

Three days later, authorities heard about the burial. They got the family to agree to disinterment of the body for purposes of cremation. What they found when they opened the casket was the boy's body in a sitting position, his arms pushing against the side of the casket. His clothes were blood-soaked and torn from the struggle to free himself, his fingertips shredded from clawing. A doctor determined that the young man, drunk at the time he was declared dead, probably regained consciousness some 24 hours after burial.

Despite Communism, the desire for traditional burials with Buddhist or Taoist pomp, drums, cymbals and crackling fireworks to scare off evil spirits, remains. Bereaved family members still select auspicious gravesites according to portents of wind and water. They dress in sackcloth, leaving their hair unkempt. Professional wailers are hired to accompany the funeral procession and ancestor worship still takes place.

As it has since the Qin Dynasty, Quingming (Day of the Dead) finds thousands attempting to invoke goodwill among departed family members by helping them to enjoy the spirit world. Offerings of food, wine, flowers, toy automobiles and furniture, cardboard computers and paper television sets are given in exchange for blessings of good fortunes from the dead. Rolls of bank notes are burned to insure that the spirits have the means for a comfortable afterlife—all this despite the prohibition of such acts, especially the burning of money.

Free of Communist-inspired restrictions on religious practices like those of China, Japan has been heavily influenced by both Buddhist and Shinto teachings. Japanese death customs and beliefs reflect that. Buddhism was brought to Japan from China around 710 AD. Buddhist temples included cemeteries that rented out family plots for burial. Buddhist monks would conduct funeral services at the family home for a fee, one of their sole sources of income. Forty-nine days later, the cremated remains of the deceased would be taken to a vault for burial below the family's single stone marker. An ornately lettered wooden board called a sotoba was all that individualized the burial spot.

Three times each year families would visit the

gravesite. Visits were also made on the first, third and seventeenth anniversaries of the death. Each visit required the purchase of a new sotoba and a donation to the temple. Responsibility for such upkeep and giving was passed on from father to son.

This tradition, dating back to the (Tokugawa) Edo Period (1603–1867), reflects the traditional Japanese practice of arranged marriages and obedience to the husband. Women did not have separate plots for burial, even when divorced. They were always buried in their husband's family plot.

As more Japanese divorce, and women become more liberated, the tradition is changing. A survey among Japanese women found that one in three preferred burial away from their husbands and in-laws. "Purchasing the grave was my ultimate resistance," said a 58-year-old woman who felt it "psychologically impossible" to contemplate burial in a common grave with her mother-in-law.

Buddhist priests in Japan worry that the loss of a single-family plot will mean loss of revenue for them. Sotobas are being replaced with copper statuettes that last longer. Land shortage is another concern. And the Shinto belief that one's ancestors are deities worthy of worship may be less viable if the prescribed family role surrounding death and burial is altered by women seeking an independent form of afterlife.

Like the Buddhists, Hindus believe in cremation. When Rajiv Gandhi, son of Indira Gandhi and grandson of Jawaharlal Nehru, was assassinated, his 20-year-old son, Rahul, lit the funeral pyre. The body was wrapped in a white shroud, white being the color symbolic of mourning in India, and in China as well.

Sandalwood is often used by Hindus for the cremation. Herbs are applied to mask the smell of burning flesh.

In addition, camphor and incense and holy water from the sacred Ganges River are applied by family members to the body of the deceased as part of the cremation process.

As with other Hindus, the people of Nepal believe that those who die are reborn into a form befitting the conduct of their previous lives. A festival called Gaj Yatra (Procession of the Cows), celebrates death, but only after the traditional thirteen days of mourning have passed.

In Bali, death is viewed as a joyous occasion, representing new beginnings, a better life through reincarnation, and possible attainment of the ultimate goal of nirvana where reincarnation ends in oneness with the universe. Accordingly, the funeral procession is a lively one. Relatives and friends happily transport the shrouded body to the cremation site on a heavily decorated tower. There the body is transferred from the tower to the symbolic animal-shaped funeral pyre or coffin. For a soldier the pyre/coffin might be a deer, for a king a winged lion. Each coffin is fashioned from a hollow tree, each adorned with brightly colored cloth and richly embossed metal, and each cremated along with the body.

If the body does not burn completely, the torso may be broken up into smaller segments. This is done with bamboo sticks. When the corpse is finally reduced to ashes, those ashes are collected and returned to the elements of a river or the sea.

Early man is said to have believed that spirits could not cross water and that ghosts would fall in if they tried to do so. During the Middle Ages, water on the floor notified those who entered that someone had died. In Biblical times the pouring of water expressed guilt or remorse. It is believed that some Jewish death customs may harken back to these ancient practices. Whatever their origins, respect and dignity remain the hallmarks of Jewish death rituals.

Jewish cemeteries always provide water so that the

living might cleanse themselves of impurities contracted from contact with the dead. Because washing of the hands symbolizes a washing of the entire body, something that only the living and not the dead may do, water is often provided at the homes of the grieving as well.

Because blood is considered to be a part of the body under Jewish law, embalming is seldom done. Autopsies must be approved by family members and are performed only when absolutely necessary. Cremation is also discouraged, based on the Biblical phrase " for dust thou art and to dust shalt thou return."

Orthodox Jews bury their dead within 24 hours of death, circumstances permitting. Until then the body is often watched over by a shomer (the Hebrew word for guard). Shomers were originally assigned to guard the deceased from evil spirits or ghosts by reading psalms to uplift them. Shomers now reflect simple regard for the dead, just as discouragement of autopsy and embalming do.

Unlike the Egyptians and other civilizations who buried their dead with possessions for the afterlife, Jews believe that:

In the hour of man's departure from this world neither silver nor gold nor precious stones nor pearls . . . but only the Torah and good works.[3]

Accordingly, the body is wrapped in a simple and inexpensive shroud of cotton or muslin, symbolizing that rich and poor are alike before God. Pockets for worldly possessions are deliberately omitted from such shrouds, called tachrichim in Hebrew. Once varied in color, all are now white to symbolize purity. Some choose to be buried in a kittel, which is similar to a shroud in design but different in having been worn during one's lifetime for holidays or special services.

There are several reasons why Jewish coffins are

made of wood rather than other materials such as metal. One is that wood decomposes quickly and allows the corpse to return to dust. Unlike metal, wood does not symbolize war but rather the trees that hid Adam and Eve when God first called them from the Garden of Eden. Finally, wood is not ostentatious but rather simple, in the Jewish tradition.

Those who mourn the dead may tear their garments, a ritual known as a k-riah. If a parent has died, the lapel is torn on the left side, closest to the heart of the surviving child. For the death of a son or daughter, sibling or spouse, the lapel is torn on the right. Usually it is the rabbi who does the tearing but among Orthodox Jews, one woman will tear the garment of another to insure modesty. Newlyweds delay mourning, and therefore the wearing and tearing of the garments for one week following their nuptials.

In Israel, where coffins are not always used, the shrouded corpse may be lowered into a hole lined with bricks. Mourners pass a shovel and take turns throwing dirt into the grave. What follows depends upon the customs adopted by the family.

A week of mourning by the bereaved family follows the funeral. It is called shivah, meaning seven days. During this time of social withdrawal, bathing is allowed only for purposes of cleanliness but not for enjoyment. Grains of sand may be placed in one's shoes (which cannot be leather because that is too comfortable) to remind one of the conditions of bereavement.

During the period of shivah, mirrors may be covered to deflect vanity, to keep prayers from being said in front of them (which is prohibited), or to keep the mourner from reflecting an uncomplimentary image of God. The custom first developed among the ancients who feared that the reflection of their soul in a mirror or water would allow ghosts to snatch it away. Candles burn throughout the seven-day period of shivah to illuminate the soul's journey toward heaven. In deference to the grieving, conversation is kept to a minimum. Mourners often sit on stools or hassocks rather than chairs, symbolic of the desire to be near the now-buried loved one.

Twelve months after burial the formal period of mourning ends with the dedication of a tombstone. Each year thereafter a candle is lit in memory of the deceased. At that time, memories of the dead are shared by loved ones.

Jewish ideas on an afterlife vary widely—from Jewish mystics, who believe in reincarnation, to Reform Jews, some of whom have eliminated the concept of resurrection from their texts. Left open to speculation is the passage referring to the Lord "reviving all." Those accepting of an afterlife base their belief on Hebrew texts which promise resurrection for all when the Messiah comes "Lord mighty, you revive the dead . . . you have endowed us with immortal life . . . bestow eternal life upon the dead."

Some Jews believe that the most pious will be resurrected first, their bodies having rolled underground to the Holy Land. To avoid that potential journey, those who can often request burial in Israel. If that is not possible, earth from the Holy Land may be placed in the coffin to further one's travels in that direction.

In Hebrew, what lies beyond death, the unknown, is called Sheol, which variously refers to the underworld abode of the dead, a subterranean region clothed in thick darkness (the return from which is impossible), the place of departed spirits, or simply the grave. It is the same definition given for the Greek Hades, a word sometimes used interchangeably with the Christian Hell.

Jewish death customs have been praised for their straightforward approach, which allows survivors to move on with life. The refusal to cosmetize a body, leaving it in a natural state for burial, some feel, lessens denial on the part of the living who are forced to face reality but who likewise benefit from the ongoing community support provided by such well-defined death practices.

Like Jews and early Christians, devout Moslems practice a "dust to dust" burial policy. Coffins often consist of simple wooden frames with top and bottom nailed on. The unembalmed corpse is washed by family members before being placed in the casket. It is wrapped in a shroud for burial. Burial takes place within 24 hours of the death, with orientation of the grave being toward the holy city of Mecca, located in Saudi Arabia. There is no cosmetizing or viewing of the body. The body is considered to be a source of vanity and therefore unimportant.

Women are believed by Moslems to have a special place in the afterlife, which is viewed as spiritual rather than physical. Therefore, they are not allowed to attend their husbands' funerals. American-born Queen Noor, who married King Hussein and became Queen of Jordan following the tragic death of Queen Alia, later admitted to disobeying that custom when her husband's funeral was held. She observed the ceremony out of sight, removed from the all-male attendees allowed at traditional Islamic funerals.

Unless for political reasons, suicide among Moslems is taboo. However, if one elects to die in a jihad (an act of holy war for the cause of Islam), access to heaven is guaranteed. For reasons similar to those described in the Jewish religion, cremation is not practiced in the Moslem faith.

For wealthy Moslems, cemetery plots may include residential caretakers who tend to the villa-like mausoleums of brick and stucco fashioned to house the dead. In Cairo's City of The Dead, an estimated 400,000 people inhabit 100,000 tombs, many illegally rather than as designated caretakers. Some caretaker families have lived among the dead for several generations. Their presence has spawned the construction of a post office, schools and a medical clinic within the confines of the City of the Dead itself. But as one caretaker of a 16th-century tomb there noted, with the coming of electricity the ghosts have disappeared.

According to their holy book, the Koran, on the Last Day of Judgment devout Moslems will witness the opening of graves as men are called to account by their god, Allah. Those who have assiduously remained humble, God-fearing and charitable in both thought and deed will live forever in the Garden of Paradise. There, on silken cushions beside flowing streams, men will enjoy "the company of dark-eyed maidens and wives of perfect purity."

Nineteenth-century burial of Moslems in Turkey seemed to reflect a preoccupation with the possible existence of vampires. A middle-aged male corpse of that era was found nailed down to his coffin with eight-inch iron spikes driven through his neck, pelvis and ankles. And while it was not uncommon for bodies to be nailed down or to be mutilated through decapitation or amputation in order to keep a suspected vampire from vacating the grave, what was unusual in this case was that Moslems had performed the ritual. Previously, it was believed that only Christians did so.

The influence of major world religions on death customs is unquestionable. So is the role of animism, sometimes classified as a primitive or early form of religion. Animism is the belief that all objects have in-dwelling souls or spirits. It also has to do with the activity of ghosts.

Some Eskimos who practice animism place a dog's head in the grave of a child. It is believed that the dog will lead the child to the land of the souls. Some Native

Americans cut an opening in the sole of the child's moccasin so that the child will not be led far away by evil spirits. The Annamese of Vietnam hold elaborate funeral rituals for dead whales that wash ashore. Whales are treated to the same rites as humans, including the burning of perfumes, scattering of gilded leaves and sand burial under a ceremonial shed.

In Africa, animism has had a tremendous influence. The dead, it is believed, remain among the living and must be treated with care so that they do not perpetrate acts of revenge. Illness is closely associated with witchcraft; it is possible that the dead will inflict illness upon the living as a reminder of their presence. Therefore, how the dead are buried is of utmost importance.

In some African cultures, burial might take place near one's home, alongside a roadway, under a tree, or beside a waterway (believed to be the special domain of the dead). Prior to burial, the body may be displayed in a courtyard, on a porch, or within some other shelter. Both the display of the body and the funeral preceding it can last for days or weeks. During that time, it is expected that the family of the deceased will provide food and drink for anyone calling upon them, including passing strangers. Prayers for the dead must be offered only at ancestral altars, never at the gravesite. Part of the death ritual involves an exchange of gifts among tribal members in order to purge themselves of past quarrels. In addition to sharing remains of the sacrifices made for the dead, participants might also dance, as well as perform lamentations of the deceased's deeds. If possible, a son or elder tribesman should also enact a symbolic attack on the house of the person who has died.

Not until it is certain that the spirit cannot rejoin the body does the period of mourning begin. That mourning could last anywhere from months to as much as 20 years, depending on the status of the deceased.

One often misunderstood aspect of animism is the issue of sacrifice and cannibalism. If one believes that all objects have a soul or spirit, then it would logically follow that ingestion of the object, or symbol thereof, could bestow powers of the dead soul upon the living. Christian communion represents just such a symbolic act of faith. So, too, does the Buddhist practice of "sky burial."

Among the Yanamamo of New Guinea, cremation of the dead is followed one year later by a ceremony in which the ashes of the deceased are consumed by kinsmen. The ashes are ground with a ceremonial mortar, decorated for male or female, and then stored in hollow gourds sealed with wax until such time as they are mixed with boiled plantain soup. Consumption of ashes from the cremated dead is considered an act of friendship and solidarity among the Yanamamo, a guarantee that their friends and relatives will again be seen. Quite a different ceremony is held for the consumption of enemy ashes, one designed to insure maximum revenge.

Preservation of skulls, bones and other body parts, as well as personal possessions belonging to the dead, is almost universal in its practice. Two thousand years before the Egyptians, the Chilean Chinchorro were mummifying their dead in the likely belief that there was some link between preserved corpses and the supernatural. Even fetuses were mummified by the Chinchorro. Why all this effort? According to researchers, ancient Andeans believed that huacas (sacred objects including mummies) could bestow fertility. Huacas were fed and clothed by the living in order to insure their participation in the fertility process. Perhaps in the belief that survival of the soul was somehow linked to survival of the body, the Inca would parade mummies of their dead rulers in much the same way that relics of Christian saints were later displayed.[4]

Italian Catholics once saved tongues cut from the mouths of martyrs. In Guatemala the scabs from the knees of Hermano Pedro, who crawled from one church to another, were preserved. On his feast day each year, the jaw of St. Anthony was paraded through the streets of Padua. Such relics symbolize, for those who believe in them, a representation of the whole.

Human desire and longing for connection to the whole is clearly reflected in rituals that honor the dead. Whether we bury or cremate, mummify or eviscerate, the intended goal remains the same—to protect the dead, to preserve their memory, and to placate ourselves through what we seek to offer them as tribute. What we do for and with the dead, and why we do it, is a clear reflection of who and what we are. We do what we do to give meaning to life, both their lives and ours.

How do we reconcile our fear of death with our basic instinctual need for some form of immortality? Perhaps by following the traditions of what those who have preceded us have done for thousands of years—practicing death customs and rituals that both confort us and affirm our sense of self. In whatever way we choose to honor the dead, not the act itself but the reasons for it are what imbue ultimate meaning to our having lived.

Chapter Seven

What Comfort And Meaning In Our Death Customs?

*Just as I choose a ship to sail in, or a house to live in,
so I choose a death for my passage from life.*
—Seneca

In our fast-moving society, where there now exists something called a "fax funeral," how relevant are death customs and rituals handed down to us from centuries past? Of what comfort are they to us? Do we even have time for death any longer, or as with so many other aspects of our personal lives, will dealing with the dead be relegated to computer chips and high-tech machines? And, should we at some point abandon our conventional approaches to human mortality, what, if any, will the emotional consequences be?

Modern communication makes cognitive escape from death's imagery a near impossibility. One week's news includes accounts of a private plane flying across the country on automatic pilot while the six passengers on board (one a world-renowned golfer), are presumed dead, their condition eerily unknowable due to heavy icing on the windows of the airplane. Eventually the plane crashes, leaving a 30-foot crater over which are scattered indiscernible bits of wreckage and debris.

That same week a commercial jetliner goes down over the Atlantic killing all 217 on board. We hear descriptions of family members who faint or cry out when told that whole bodies are not expected to be recovered from the waters of the ocean and that there may never be anything retrieved for burial.

Meanwhile, jurors condemn a teenager to 120 years in prison for having shot and killed his parents and three school classmates. Much the same sentence is applied to the perpetrator of a hate crime against a young college student, tortured and hanged scarecrow-style on a fence, where he was left to bleed to death because he was gay.

"He is, I mean, he was such a wonderful person," sobs a disbelieving older gentleman when asked about the hate-crime killing of his grandson, along with six other innocent bystanders. And by week's end, yet another media death, that of a 45-year-old former professional football player who was awaiting a liver transplant becomes the headline story.

Routinely we see news clips of body bags being removed from places like those where we work, and SWAT teams searching neighborhoods like our own. Playgrounds and churches act as backdrops for death scenes. A week later it all begins again.

Those are the deaths we hear about through the media. Aside from them, how many others take place without our knowledge? How many survivors are called upon each and every day to deal with the death of someone close to them? What percentage of those called upon have any preparation for the task? And what, if any, comfort do they find in the rituals assigned to death in our culture?

Beyond the numbing shock of death's occurrence, many survivors are overwhelmed with the immediate task of having to plan a funeral service that typically involves many major decisions within the first 24 hours. Such decisions include:

— Selection of a funeral home, if one is to be used.
— Deciding whether or not to have the body embalmed.
— Selection of burial clothes and a casket.
— Deciding on whether to have a visitation, and, if so, where and when.
— Deciding on whether to have a traditional funeral service or a memorial service, as well as where and when.
— Selection of pallbearers, music, someone to deliver a eulogy, and whatever else will be a part of the service.
— Whether to have the body buried, entombed, cremated or follow some other ritual.
— Where to direct memorial donations.
— Notification of friends and relatives.

The cost of such decisions, for many of us, constitutes the third-largest expenditure of our lives, exceeded only by housing and automobiles. Such decisions may also represent a potential source of guilt and regret for survivors who may later agonize over choices made or not made during the throes of grief.

On one of the numerous visits I made to funeral homes with my students, I inadvertently became privy to a conversation among three sisters, called upon to make funeral arrangements for their sibling. It is estimated that, on average, each of us will be involved in making funeral arrangements about once every 10 years. That statistic would seem to have applied to these women, who were shocked over how expensive they felt funerals had become.

"I had no idea that caskets cost so much," commented one sister. "Do you think she would have wanted us to spend a lot on that?" "Well I suppose we could cash in a money market certificate or a CD," suggested another. "Oh, I just wish we knew what she would have wanted," lamented a third. "Now we'll always have to wonder if we did the right thing for her."

As I listened to them discussing how best to proceed, I thought of my students and how our visits to the funeral home were but practice—preparation for the time when, like the three sisters, they would be confronted with such decisions. Like those three sisters, at the most emotionally vulnerable time of our lives we are called upon to act as practical consumers. The pitting of our sentiments against our sensibilities may result in residual doubt later during the grieving process.

We may experience what grief psychologists refer to as death guilt—those lingering doubts about whether we did the right thing, why we chose or did not choose to do a particular thing, why we failed to think of something important at the time. A guest speaker in my class described such death guilt associated with the deaths of two of her children. The first, a stillborn, she never saw. The body was simply placed in a casket and buried while she lay grief-stricken and stunned in her hospital room. As a first-time mother, she explained, she had never considered that her child could be born dead, let alone what she would want, should that worst-case scenario occur.

Years later, that same woman suffered a second tragic loss when her son died of SIDS. Her decision to place her own first-communion rosary in the child's casket resulted in later regret over not having kept it for one of her surviving children.

In the bestselling book, *Tuesdays with Morrie,* Morrie has his funeral held before he dies so that he can hear the praise and adulation most of us hope for but will never witness ourselves. Some might view such an act as egotistical and macabre, just as others might question a request by the late actor, Cary Grant, that his remains be cremated immediately following his death, sans funeral or memorial service, or Caroline Kennedy Schlossberg's decision to have her brother John's cremation remains scattered at sea rather than placed alongside the very public gravesite of their parents at Arlington National Cemetery.

The point comes down not to the outcome but to the reasons for our choices and decisions. Such reckoning with death, whether it be our own or another's, necessitates a long-term, careful analysis of our personal beliefs about life, and what, if anything, is to follow. Becoming well informed on death customs is not something we find attractive. But in considering the alternative, perhaps it is something we should take time for now.

Whatever our perspective on how best to say those last goodbyes, wouldn't a well-reasoned examination of our own desires and wishes serve to assuage the doubts and regrets that haunt us when we try to pretend that death does not really occur, at least in our house? We cannot alter the facts of death but we do have the ability to decide how we choose to proceed in dealing with it. And through such choices we may affirm whatever relationship to the deceased best aids us in letting go.

Most of us have some memory of the first time we attended a visitation or a funeral, watching as people quietly filed past the casket and perhaps peered in, whispering quietly about how lifelike or peaceful the remains of the deceased seemed. We may have imagined that we could see the corpse breathe or fantasized that it would sit upright, as in horror movies we had watched, or perhaps it would let out a moan.

And during the services, while others wept over words spoken about the deceased, we may have considered whether or not we should be crying too. Most of all, we surely wondered how we would manage to get through such an ordeal, accepting condolences, seeing our loved one lying still in the casket, watching the burial or entombment of the last physical vestige of a cherished fellow human being. Little wonder, then, that the very thought of funerals evokes a feeling of empty dread and numbness in our private moments of reflection on them.

The word funeral comes from the Sanskrit, meaning smoke. In many cultures, a death ritual often involves fire. Fire and smoke have been equated with the release of the spirit or the soul from the body. That desire for release of the spirit or the soul from the body was part of our early Judeo-Christian tradition. The spirit or soul, it was believed, separated from the corpse, leaving the corpse to disintegrate into dust.

Most Early American funerals were, of necessity, stark and simple. But whatever one's circumstances, there were certain death customs that were adhered to, if possible, beginning with the death watch or death vigil. Immortalized in lithographs, such as the one done by Currier and Ives of George Washington's deathbed scene, family and friends could be found gathered about the bedside of the dying, there to glean knowledge of death through the last words of wisdom uttered by the dying. Some such lithographs were prepared in advance, leaving appropriate spaces for the deceased's name and portrait, which were added later.

Rather than lithographs, colonial artists such as Charles Wilson and Rembrandt Peale would paint post-mortem portraits of the deceased. Surrounded by such symbols of death as doves, representing messengers of God, oak leaves for adult males, full rose blooms for adult females, and rosebuds for children, the dead were remembered on canvas.

Young ladies of the early 19th century might embroider a romanticized death scene depicting mourners at the gravesite, surrounded by weeping willow trees, symbolic of both mourning and resurrection. As access to cameras became more widespread, such embroidered pieces were replaced with post-mortem photographs, oftentimes the only ones ever taken, particularly of infants and children.

The end of the deathwatch or vigil likely came about when doctors began complaining about lack of hygiene caused by curious strangers who followed clergymen into the sickroom of the dying. With it went the accepted natural intimacy between those about to die and their witnesses.

Since most people died at home, that is where the visitation and the funeral took place. A wooden plank or even a door might have had to be employed for display of the body. Sometimes the body was simply left in bed for viewing.

The average life expectancy of a 19th century male was 38.5 years, while that for a female of the 19th century was about 40.5 years. There is no formal recording of such statistics for the 18th-century. Faulty medical practices in both centuries, combined with a lack of sanitation, meant that over and over again families would face the tasks associated with death—of washing and dressing the corpse, possibly laying it out for visitation, making a casket and digging the grave.

Without embalming, putrefaction became a serious problem. The build-up of methane gasses and breakdown of tissue and fluids caused swelling of the face and distention of the body (sometimes two to three times the normal size), as well as blistering of the flesh. Within 12 to 18 hours, a corpse might be unrecognizable as hair slipped from the scalp, blood oozed from the mouth and nostrils, eyeballs liquefied, and tissue began turning to liquid. Maggots, having appeared within moments of death (as they still do), would continue their flesh-eating work throughout.[1]

Little wonder, then, that it became necessary to pass laws requiring burial so as to insure that the corpses of the disenfranchised, in various stages of decomposition, were not literally left lying about to rot. In part, those laws may have led to the establishment of undertakers. As early as 1768, a woman advertised her upholstery and undertaking services (a combination hearkening back to England) in the *New York Journal of General Advertisers.* Her inventory included shrouds, sheets and all things necessary for a proper funeral.

In 1779, Michael Jenkins of Baltimore expanded his cabinet making business to include coffins. The word coffin refers to a chest used for burial of a body. Casket is a word that originally meant a container used to hold precious items such as jewels. Although iron caskets were available by the early 1800's, most were made of wood. The type of wood used signified one's social class or station.

Understandably, cabinet and furniture makers were commonly coffin or casket makers as well. The next logical step was for them to become undertakers, which many of them did. In New York City, at the turn of the century, it cost 25 cents to purchase an undertaker's license.

When they were called to the home of someone who had died, undertakers often came equipped with a lightweight wicker casket. This casket was used to move the body from upstairs to downstairs. Some homes had a coffin or casket niche in the wall along the stairway landing. An arched indentation, the coffin or casket niche allowed the casket to be turned without causing damage to either the casket or the stairwell wall.

Downstairs the body might or might not be embalmed; but, if so, embalming was done in the kitchen. Then the washed and dressed body was placed, usually in the parlor, for viewing. A catafalque or bier was used as a stand for the casket (again, this might be a plank or door depending on what was available). It was often draped in black cloth of either crepe or velvet.

Viewing the body, also referred to as a wake or visitation, probably originated from customs related to superstition. Early peoples feared that evil spirits might enter the unwatched or unburied corpse. In the 18th-century Welsh county of Pembrokeshire, wakes included a practice called hir-wen-gwd, meaning white bag or shroud. It consisted of drawing the corpse up the chimney and slowly lowering it back into the casket. No one seems to know exactly why this was done execpt it might confuse evil spirits.[2]

Herbs and flowers have been used at funerals for centuries. Their purpose was two-fold. One reason, of course, was to mask the odor of putrefaction. The other was to slow down the putrefaction process. Rosemary, believed to help prevent rotting, was often placed inside the casket.

By the 19th century, flowers had taken on further use as symbolic arrangements for the expression of emotion. The "broken column" arrangement signified a life cut short. "Gates ajar" represented the passage of a loved one from this to another dimension. Flower pillows became popular as did arrangements made up of the number of flowers representative of the deceased person's age. Florists had wrought-iron molds which they could decorate to fashion whichever arrangement was desired.

Both 19th-century mourning dress habits and behavior were heavily influenced by Queen Victoria of
England. For 40 years following the death of her beloved
husband, Prince Albert, the Queen wore mourning clothes,
which included black bloomers.

To the ancients black represented the absence of
color. It also signified darkness and night and the absence
of joy. For at least a year or two, members of a bereaved
family were expected to wear black, then steel or pearl
gray, then purple, in that order. Men might only wear an
armband in the appropriate mourning color. Women were
expected to dress entirely in the shade appropriate to their
stage of bereavement—black for the first year, then a combination of black and white (gray), for the first half of the
second year, with purple to finish out their designated
time of mourning.

Jewelry also had to be in keeping with one's mourning status. Oftentimes, the dead were memorialized with
specially designed jewelry. Pins, bracelets, necklaces,
brooches and stickpins were not only worn by members of
the grieving family but also given to relatives and friends
as tokens of regard for the deceased.

Hair from the deceased was a popular material for
creation of such jewelry. Why hair? Dating back to at least
the Middle Ages, the custom was to take nail and hair clip-
pings from the dead in order to retain the powers of the
deceased.

While the traditional funeral service is something
that did not change markedly over the years, one thing
that has changed since Colonial times is the method of
transporting the body to its burial site. As cemeteries
became farther removed from populated areas, it was no
longer practical for people to walk in a funeral procession
from their home to the graveyard. Horse-drawn carriages

and a hearse replaced the foot-procession of mourners, six of whom had previously walked with a casket balanced on their shoulders.

The word hearse originally referred to a spiked candelabrum used over a coffin. Later it referred to a structure built over and around the coffin, to which memorial verses and epitaphs written by friends of the dead were attached. That structure evolved into a platform on which to transport the coffin. Eventually, the hearse was equipped with wheels and the coffin was horse-drawn rather than carried on the shoulder of pallbearers.

Livery stables began to specialize in providing black horses bedecked with black plumes, false manes and tails, and blackened hooves for funeral processions. Sometimes livery stable owners became undertakers too.

Following World War I, more and more people moved to urban areas where many became apartment dwellers and often knew their neighbors less well. As the pace of life accelerated, the amount of time available for families to devote to making funeral preparations declined. That combination of circumstances led to widespread use of funeral homes, adding another layer of insulation from the realities and intimacies of death to people's lives.

It followed that early 20th-century obituaries and eulogies also became less personalized and emotionally charged than they had been in the 1800's. Some blamed the sheer number of deaths caused by World War I for depersonalizing funeral rituals. Whatever the causes, those intimate relationships with death so evident in 18th- and 19th-century America gave way to less elaborate, more sterile approaches.

At 96 percent of all American funerals today there is an open casket, which means that about 96 percent of the dead are embalmed. Embalming the corpse, dressing it and applying cosmetics to it for a viewing are psychologically helpful to survivors, say many funeral directors. Seeing the corpse in a more presentable way may help replace the imagery of a loved one ravaged by disease or battered or mutilated in some way.

When asked about the practice of embalming, one funeral director described an incident where a family asked him to handle arrangements for their daughter who had been decapitated in a widely publicized accident. The child's parents were particularly concerned over how a closed casket might affect their daughter's friends and schoolmates. It was left to the mortician to make her presentable, which he was able to do. For that family, an open casket was preferable.

When families are asked about whether or not to have an open casket, they often assume that saying yes will assure that the body will look better than their last memory of it. "We can't work miracles though," cautioned one funeral director who noted that families often become upset when their expectations collide with reality.

In cases of extreme trauma to the body, that funeral director would ask the family if they would care to view the deceased before deciding on an open or closed casket, because what they may be showing him in a picture of the loved one may not be "what I have just seen when I looked at the corpse," he said. Almost always in such cases, he said, the family would agree to look at the deceased before making their decision. Never, said the funeral director, had a family come back to him later to say that they regretted their decision, no matter how difficult the viewing process had been for them.

Issues of embalming, cosmetizing and dressing of the corpse perhaps go to the question of just who funerals are held for, the living or the dead. On the side of the living would be the woman who took great exception to the fact that part of the cosmetizing procedure done on her grandfather involved trimming his nasal and ear hairs. "Why would you do that," she asked, "when it alters the way we remember him?"

Those, like film star Clara Bow, might seem to weigh in more on the side of funerals being for the dead. It was she who requested that her casket be lined in an eggshell-color silk or satin so as not to clash with the negligee she would be wearing. Bella Lugosi was buried in his Dracula attire, complete with make-up. Richard Burton asked to be buried in his lucky red socks. The truth is that one can be dressed (or not), to whatever taste or degree one specifies.

Casket selection, unless prearranged, is often a task left to the living. It is worth noting that some funeral homes merchandise caskets, many of which have as much as a 500 percent markup, so that the viewer sees the most expensive ones first and may, in some cases, be denied access to the least-costly ones unless requested.

Certain caskets are advertised as being airtight and warranted for some 50–100 years against leakage if they are properly constructed. Some come equipped with innerspring mattresses. It was rumored that Christian Science founder Mary Baker Eddy asked for a working telephone in hers.

Caskets may be customized as to color and design, both inside and out. A recent trend was the use of professional league football colors on caskets. They can also be made longer and/or wider for taller or heavier people.

One funeral director said that during a funeral home open house, an adult midget approached him with concerns over what kind of casket he might be able to have. Not wanting a child's casket, he was assured that a custom-sized adult casket could be made for him.

In cases where people are too heavy for even an oversized casket, it may be necessary to use a grave box as a casket. Such was the case for a man who weighed nearly 700 pounds. His viewing was confined to immediate family members because he had to be laid out on two adjoining funeral home dressing tables roped together, then placed directly into the concrete grave box at the cemetery.

Baby caskets are usually lightweight and appear to be made of molded plastic. In cases of miscarriage or a stillborn birth, it is up to the family to decide what to do with the remains as far as services and disposal are concerned.

In cases of death caused by accident, funeral directors said that the casket selected more often was chosen for comfort, with little concern for cost. In instances of suicide, a basic casket was more often selected. Why? Possibly it had to do with residual anger and resentment toward the deceased.

The practice of holding a visitation (also referred to as a wake or vigil), has evolved into an opportunity for the living to express condolences to the bereaved and to pay their respects to the dead. When asked how funeral customs have changed over the years, one funeral director brought up the visitation. It has become a social occasion, he said, "with people wandering in and out, some carrying cans of soda. . . . People seldom cry anymore. In fact, they don't even look at what's lying in the box."

Another funeral director described visitations he had conducted for recent immigrants from Eastern Europe as being quite the opposite. At the visitation, family members are seated in hierarchical order near the casket and each is paid the appropriate respects by those filing by, he said. Failure to abide by such protocol is considered an extreme insult, warranting physical confrontation, and in some instances an altercation.

Probably the most extreme example of change with regard to visitations is the drive-up window concept. The casket is placed on display behind a window and mourners pay respects as they drive past, never leaving their vehicles.

Nowadays, visitations are frequently held just prior to the funeral services. As fewer people remain affiliated with a particular church or temple, more and more visitations and funerals are held at the funeral home itself. In reality, funeral services may be conducted almost anywhere. A funeral home in the western United States shows funeral services live on the Internet to family members who cannot attend. All that is required to log on is a passcode provided by the funeral home.

A growing alternative to the standard funeral service is called a memorial service. It may be held weeks or months after the death has occurred. The purpose of a memorial service is to celebrate the life of the deceased. The body of the deceased is usually not present at a memorial service. Often, burial or cremation precedes the memorial service with only family members and perhaps a few close friends in attendance.

There tends to be a less formal atmosphere at memorial services. Friends and family are asked to share favorite memories and stories, perhaps to hold hands while singing or praying, and possibly to participate in a group activity such as the releasing of balloons or the planting of a tree in memory of the departed.

Planning one's own funeral or memorial service can be a sobering experience. It can also be a source of great comfort and satisfaction. More and more frequently, according to funeral directors, people are requesting personalized services, which include photo displays alongside the casket, country-western or blues instead of organ music, personal items of a sporting or hobby nature next to the body in the casket, and gravestones etched with career or pleasure-related images. Some even record audio and/or videotapes of themselves to be played at the funeral.

The Federal Trade Commission regulates funeral practices to a certain degree by requiring that the consumer be informed, step-by-step, of what is being purchased and at what cost. One funeral director noted that the biggest change experienced in his East-coast business, which had been run by members of his family for nearly 100 years, was the "shopping around" mentality on the part of consumers. "They will call and ask us to begin making arrangements," he said, "but when we go to pick up the body we're told it's already been taken to another funeral home." His theory on why this is happening has to do with the breakdown of the nuclear family. Where once there was loyalty to a particular funeral home, now a live-in or a significant other may decide that they can do "better than your prices." And because more and more families no longer recognize or follow a head of household, there isn't the tradition of returning to the funeral home that took care of grandpa and grandma and maybe even the generations preceding them.

Discount funeral homes are becoming increasingly common. Cost-cutting casket suppliers can now be found in strip malls. It's actually possible to conduct a low-cost, do-it-yourself funeral if you are willing to transport a casket from the death scene to where it will be buried. For some people this is an alternative that is both practical, as far as cost, and appealing in the personal approach it allows one to take with the care of the dead.

As with all aspects of death, most of us imagine ourselves attending, or at least looking down upon, our own funeral. Consciously or not, we may plan our lives in a way that insures a heavily attended funeral with widespread tributes and long-lasting memorials to follow. The desire to have one's name in the history books is what Robert J. Lifton may have meant by the "creative mode" of immortality.

At least fleetingly, we probably all fear an unattended, impersonal funeral service. Certainly we fear an unacknowledged death. That is why many people choose to plan their own funeral or memorial services. Winston Churchill did. He referred to the detailed arrangements as "Operation Hope Not." Society maven, Babe Paley, had an elegant luncheon planned for guests attending her funeral. Said a friend, "It was as if she were there."

However we wish to leave this world is, as Malcolm Forbes once said, "very personal." To the extent that our exit glorifies, dignifies or vilifies our lives may matter a great deal to us, or not at all. To the extent that it comforts those who survive us may be of greater concern.

What will be spoken of us when we die? How will we be remembered, memorialized, honored? Whether effusive or inconsequential, generic or germane, our passage from the land of the living to that of the dead, how ever fashioned, reflects the reality of our once having been alive. The answers to those questions, therefore, are not to be found in our death, but rather in the day-to-day conduct of our lives.

Chapter Eight

So What's To Become Of What Remains When We Die?

All compound things are subject to decay; work out your end with diligence.

—Aristotle

The notion of who we really are, as reflected in our personal choices surrounding death, reverberated in the comment made by a friend inquiring as to the content of this book. "It deals with issues related to human mortality and their impact on the quality of our lives," I said. To which he responded, "Oh, you mean fire or maggots?" How much more succinctly could he have phrased it?

What our own death signifies to us is mirrored in the method of body disposal that we choose. One need only think back to the approaches adopted by other cultures to understand that. Each cultural approach stands as a clear testament to how physical death is perceived as well as to what has preceded it—and what, if anything, will follow. Whether the body is buried or burned, protected from decay or deliberately exposed to it, such determinations and the rituals attendant to them affirm who we are and what we believe.

As we struggle to integrate the realities of death into our conscious being, a single element of that process—relegation of the remains, the body, the corpse—may disconcert us like no other. We are called upon to redirect our dependencies upon what has been to us a life, a presence, a unique and irreplaceable being, and now focus upon the pedestrian task of disposal—of what to do with this last physical vestige that we have recognized and loved and now must surrender. What was once to us a parent, a child, a sibling, a mate, a friend, is irreversibly transformed into an inanimate object requiring no more of us than simply to discard it. How can it be?

How are we to protect, comfort, and safeguard that which is no longer the person we knew? And how do we integrate the process into our ongoing lives? Is it possible for the human mind to accept such a radical and wrenching occurrence? It is in response to just these dilemmas that we make our choices.

For the majority of people in this country, traditional in-ground burial remains the preferred method of body disposal. Influenced by Judeo-Christian religious beliefs, in-ground burial likewise provided a practical way to handle death, which occurred at times and in places where no alternative might exist.

Early graves were often so shallow that body parts might be seen protruding from them. If the ground were too hard or too frozen, or the deceased too poor to afford proper burial, the corpse might not be buried at all. Legislation had to be enacted to insure that human remains were, in fact, buried rather than literally left by the side of the road.

By contrast, those wealthy enough to afford it might choose to be buried in lead-lined coffins. A prominent industrialist from our local community chose just that, the lead-lined vault being double-locked and placed inside a mausoleum.

Aside from issues of preservation, the advantages of such interments come from information gained if and when exhumation takes place. Bodies preserved in lead-lined coffins or vaults may reveal useful information about the diet, disease, and general physical conditions of the deceased.

An example is evidence of malaria, endemic to earlier generations, that was found in the well-preserved corpse of a privileged colonial matron, buried in a lead-lined coffin, for over 300 years. Recent speculation that malaria may have saved Rome from pillage by Attila the Hun is based on the unearthing of Roman corpses which, after centuries, still contain vestiges of that dreaded disease, a disease said to be greatly feared by the barbarian invader.

Unless one is buried in a lead-lined vault, it cannot be assumed that the corpse will be entirely protected underground. A sealed vault inside a concrete grave box or liner certainly offers some insulation from water, tree roots, heaving of the ground and other elements of deterioration. But issues of time and the elements remain.

Each of us has wondered what really happens to a body once it is buried. How long does it remain intact? What would it look like 50 to 100 years later? Are the ghoulish images of corpses from horror pictures really accurate depictions?

During my years of teaching I often heard funeral directors and cemetery supervisors respond to questions regarding the condition of bodies buried for various lengths of time and under various conditions. My personal curiosity about witnessing an actual disinterment was partly that, curiosity—perhaps going back to childhood when several of us buried a dead squirrel in a coffee can for three weeks and then dug it up—but it centered more on wanting to be able to answer questions asked of me on the subject as honestly and accurately as I could.

A disinterment in the cemetery where I serve as commissioner provided the chance for me to witness such a procedure. It was with permission of the family who had ordered the disinterment that I was present.

Disinterments are not an easy nor a particularly pleasant thing to watch, as I discovered. But sometimes they become necessary—for medical reasons; to further investigate cause of death; for identification purposes; to make certain that the person purportedly buried at the site is indeed that person; or for family reasons, including the wish to have remains reinterred alongside other family members or in another location.

The purpose of this particular disinterment was to move the body of the deceased from her grave of some 40 years to a family mausoleum that had been recently constructed. It was her son who, having had the mausoleum built, observed the procedure along with a funeral director, several cemetery workers, and myself.

Opening the grave required some backhoe work, which, when completed, revealed the top of a cement grave box. As the grave box was lifted from its resting place, a sloshing sound could be heard. The grave box was filled with water.

Resting inside the grave box was the casket which showed extensive signs of water damage from having been afloat. Carefully, it was placed on the ground. As the cemetery workers began to empty water from the grave box, a distinctly unpleasant odor filled the air.

At that point, the funeral director stepped forward and gingerly opened the casket. As he did so, more water was released. It dripped from the shreds of lining still clinging to the casket lid.

Emotion overtook each of us as we watched the son approach and gaze on the remains of his mother, whom he had buried so many years before. As he did so, he wept and spoke quietly to her. At that moment, his feelings and thoughts, memories and reflections were his alone. Whatever they might have been, for the rest of us standing there, all we could do was silently witness his response to a waterlogged casket holding the remains of his beloved mother.

Her face was covered with something called adipocere. Soapy in appearance, it is a waxy, brownish substance produced by the exposure of fat and muscle to excessive moisture, even when, as in this case, the body was embalmed. The corpse was carefully transferred to a body bag or pouch made of rubber, which was heavily treated with a disinfecting powder designed to absorb moisture and odor. The body, inside the body bag, was eventually placed in a new casket for entombment in the mausoleum.

Remarkably, the burial clothes appeared in good condition, despite being visibly wet. A brooch could be seen attached to one shoulder of the late 1940's style dress. One shoe was missing but the other, again of that era, remained.

I later asked this man why he had chosen to have his family's remains relocated to a mausoleum. He explained that it gave him a sense of doing something for the dead, an act of gratitude and respect. Following the death of his father, while he himself was still a child, his mother, he said, had struggled to support him and his brother. She had been aided by an uncle who assumed the role of their adopted father. "I have been blessed," he told me. "Now I want to share that, to have the ones I love—my father and mother, my uncle—those who made it possible to be here together, safe and protected, the way they always made me feel."

Whether he realized it or not, his longing to protect in such a way hearkened back to the creation of the first mausoleum, built as a tomb for King Mausolus c. 353 BC. It was built as a tribute of love by his devoted wife, a tribute from whose name we derive the word mausoleum, a tribute that became one of the Seven Wonders of the Ancient World. Likewise, there is the Taj Mahal in India, commissioned by Shah Jahan as a burial site befitting the beauty of his beloved wife, who died following the birth of their 12th child. Considered to be one of the most perfect architectural structures in existence, it was designed as a tomb where the Shah could lie eternally at his love's side.

Mausoleums were, and are, designed and built to safeguard against the elemental ravages more likely to occur with in-ground burial. But the degrees to which they can preserve and protect a body are limited. Even one as elaborate as that found in Brooklyn's Green Wood Cemetery, outfitted with its own private heating system, cannot totally stave off the inevitable.

While the cost of constructing an individual mausoleum lies beyond the pale for most of us, above-ground crypts offer a less expensive alternative. They may be either indoor or outdoor, indoor being pricier due to increased maintenance costs created by extra upkeep. As might be expected, both are susceptible to insect infestations.

Crypts are generally priced according to whether they are at eye-level (considered most desirable and thus most costly), and whether they are "side-by-side," "true companion" (where the head of one coffin touches the toe

SO WHAT'S TO BECOME OF WHAT REMAINS WHEN WE DIE?   121

of the other), or "stacked." There are also abby crypts that are partially below ground at the bottom of the crypt complex. Crypts are occasionally built as high-rises. One such example in the South is a vast building of several stories.

Crypt and mausoleum entombments are rather simple to do. The casket is raised or lowered to the appropriate level on a lift. A mechanism then slides the casket into place, after which a tablet (usually of granite), is clipped into place over the face of the opening.

In order to be placed in either type of crypt, the corpse must be embalmed. Crypts are often selected in the belief that the corpse will be preserved indefinitely. That is not entirely true. Under dry conditions the corpse tends to mummify. But before that takes place, liquid and gasses from the body are released. To accommodate the liquids, a form of "drip pan" is required to be placed under the casket by some mausoleums and crypts. Ventilation pipes dispense odors caused by the release of gasses.

In places like New Orleans, where the ground is water-laden and soggy, above-ground crypt burial is clearly preferable. During heavy flooding several years ago, caskets were found floating down the Mississippi River. Caskets sometimes include a tubular device with the name, date of birth and death, and other relevant information to provide possible identification under such circumstances.

At the cemetery where I serve as a commissioner, there are a number of mausoleums and outdoor crypts. Recently I was called upon to help determine how best to proceed with replacement of a granite crypt face that had been dislocated due to settling of outside mausoleum walls. What was visible inside the crypt were the desiccated remains of a gentleman dressed in a black frock coat. His hands and face appeared leather-like, much as the skin of a mummy. Because the crypt ran lengthwise, his left shoulder faced outward. Absent from the shoulder socket was an arm, which had separated and fallen away. What remained of the casket was a collection of dried shards and splintered wood. Above the exposed crypt, on shelves designed for that purpose, rested two bronze urns containing the cremation remains of this gentleman's family members. It struck me that the dried shards and wood splinters below bore a striking resemblance to what remains following cremation.

Many people refer to cremation remains as ashes, which they are not. What they are are bone fragments, pulverized to a degree that would make them generally unidentifiable. These fragments vary slightly in color and size, most being small, grayish-white objects with an appearance somewhere between sea coral and aged wood.

In her will, my mother directed that her body be cremated. "You girls won't be coming here to visit a grave," she said, "and besides, I've always hated being cold. Scatter my remains on my pastureland, among the hills that I love. But don't put me in the ground."

As her death drew near, the task of accompanying my stepfather to the funeral home to arrange that cremation fell to me. His selection of an expensive oak casket for her seemed a tender attempt at providing the only protection he felt he could, against a form of body disposal not of his choosing.

Following her funeral, he and I stood together, watching that casket being loaded into the hearse for the 50-mile drive to the crematory. I knew his thoughts and feelings differed from mine but what was important at that moment was not our personal viewpoints. It was rather what we shared—an abiding comfort born of the knowledge that we had done as she had wished.

Once forbidden by the Catholic and Jewish faiths, cremation is now chosen as a method of body disposal by nearly 25 percent of those living in the United States. In the West the number is about 60 percent, in the Midwest about 17 percent and in the South slightly lower. Far less expensive than either above or in-ground burial, cremation does require that the body be held for 48 hours after death to insure adequate time for an investigation of causes, should there be such a need.

At the crematory, the corpse is placed in a furnace called a retort. Most crematories (and/or state laws) require that the body be in some sort of container, even if it is just a cardboard box. Inside the retort, gas or oil flames are used to produce the 2,500 degree temperature required for the cremation process.

That process may take anywhere from two to several hours, depending on the size of the body and what kind of container it is in. Sometimes the casket lid is removed to accelerate the process. Once the casket has burned away, which happens rather rapidly unless it is made of metal, the body itself is exposed to heat so intense that it causes rapid oxidation as moisture is evaporated.

Hair and skin are the first to burn away, followed by muscle, internal organs, until finally what remains is skeletal bone. For an average-sized adult, that bone would weigh somewhere between three and seven pounds.

During the course of a cremation, which may be witnessed by family members upon request, crematory staff workers perform a task called stoking. It involves using a long metal pole to move the corpse around, thus insuring maximum and more even oxidation. Once the retort has cooled down, the remains are swept together and any metal fragments from the casket or other sources are removed with a magnet.

The bone fragment remains are then pulverized, as previously mentioned, packaged and labeled for return to either the funeral home or the family of the deceased. From there it becomes a personal decision as far as what will follow. There actually are no legal restrictions on what may be done with cremation remains.

Some are never claimed by relatives and remain sitting on funeral home shelves or entombed with other unclaimed remains in a crypt purchased for that purpose by the funeral home. More often they are either scattered or buried or entombed, following a service of some kind. They may be placed in a commemorative memorial garden area or interred on top of a previously buried casket. There are also small crypts called columbariums, structures designed with glass or bronze-covered niches to accommodate urns in which cremation remains have been placed. It was the Romans who first used columbariums. They were seen as places where the living could offer food and flowers to the souls of the dead.

While scattering the cremation remains of my mother, as she had asked me to do, I was filled with thoughts and feelings, memories and recollections as personal to me as those of the gentleman who had had his mother's remains moved to a mausoleum. It was then that I encountered a rather sizable fragment of her skull, which had somehow not been pulverized. Holding it in my hands gave me a sense of comfort that I cannot explain. Nothing about her death was altered by my having it. Its sole purpose was as a reminder of the utter fragility and finitude of life, of how quickly and irrevocably the joys derived from human association and companionship are reduced, and once again, why each moment of our existence should be treasured.

Among the Tibetans, who view our bodies as nothing more than disposable receptacles in which we briefly reside, the skull is often kept and decorated with gold or silver, for those very reasons, to tangibly represent the transitory nature of being human. As do they, I chose to keep that portion of my mother's skull and to reflect upon it.

There are those who, quite unlike the Tibetans, subscribe to the notion of total body preservation, which is called cryonics. They believe that at some as yet undetermined time in the future, technology will provide a means of regenerating life in a frozen corpse. According to Robert Ettinger, president of the Cryonics Institute and author of the book, *The Prospect of Immortality*, cryonics works as follows:

> *The patient is placed on a heart-lung resuscitator immediately after death. Breathing and circulation are artificially restored. The body is packed in ice and sent to a cryonics lab. Blood is replaced with protective chemicals called cryoprotectants, which are antifreeze compounds such as glycerol to reduce or prevent ice formation. Rubbing alcohol and dry ice are used to chill the body to minus 110° Farenheit, and it is wrapped in an insulated bag. The body is placed in a double-insulated stainless steel tank filled with liquid nitrogen and kept at minus 320°. The tank is tilted with the head down in case the nitrogen level accidentally drops and thawing begins. Tanks are monitored daily by staff members who check the temperatures.*[1]

Current costs for cryonics range anywhere from $28,000 at Ettinger's institute to $120,000 at a California facility that also freezes just heads.

The concept of freezing just the head has created some controversy, not least of which centers on how and when the head may be removed from the body. Thomas Donaldson, a terminally ill California mathematician, was refused the right to have his head severed (before death occurred), by the state's superior courts. In another case, the son of a woman whose head was severed for freezing was investigated for having possibly proceeded with the decapitation before death had actually occurred.

Over a thousand people belong to cryonics groups, 400 of them wishing to be frozen upon death. At least 26 bodies are currently frozen at one of the three known cryonics institutes: Trans Time Inc. in Oakland, California; Alcor in Scottsdale, Arizona; or Ettinger's Cryonics Institute in Oak Park, Michigan. For years, Walt Disney was reported to be listed among them, but both his family and Forest Lawn spokespersons insist that his remains are located at Forest Lawn.

Arguments in favor of cryonics emphasize the "magical" possibility of extended life through future revival. Says one advocate, "It's not that I want to come back, it's that I don't want to die." Those opposed to cryonics view it as "a kind of narcissism," placing "too much value on mortal life . . . a contradiction to the Christian belief of resurrection." Ettinger had this to say about the practice of cryonics:

> Death is a matter of degree, depending on the state of medical technology. I think most of us want to come back as soon as it's technically possible.[2]

For those wishing to donate their bodies to science, neither the issue of body disposal nor its possible revival are concerns. In many states, donated bodies are heavily embalmed to preserve them until such time as the family is certain about sanctioning release. The time period in some states for holding the corpse is two years. Once relegated to the status of cadaver, the body may be dissected for any number of scientific research purposes. Whatever remains following the dissection is cremated.

And then there are the rather exotic alternative methods of disposal which include mummification, taxidermy, exposure of the dead body, or having it freeze-dried. Native Americans of the plains once used exposure as a method of disposing of their dead. The buffalo or deerskin-wrapped corpse was baked by the sun as it lay atop a platform or among the branches of a tree. Even today, Zoroastrians hold to their 6th-century belief in exposure as an alternative to putrefying the earth by burying corpses within it. But despite the advantages of no cost and the conservation of space, exposure is not a legal form of body disposal in this country.

Lack of interest, rather than issues of legality, have hindered the use of human taxidermy. Once offered at a cost of over $2,000 by Schoepfer Studios in New York, the process involves removal of the eyes, which are replaced with glass ones. The corpse is gutted and the flesh scraped off along with body fat, both of which are "pickled" to achieve a form of human leather. The skin is then stretched and sewn around a human form.

In 1986, Jeff Weber of Pinellas Park, Florida, purchased a freeze-dry chamber for $30,000 to launch his business, Preservation Specialties, the only freeze-drying mortuary in the world at that time. Having serviced birds, hamsters, reptiles, cats and dogs, Weber said he would soon move into the "human sector." His charges, based on the size of the object to be freeze-dried, ranged from $400 to $1,800 for animals and $20,000 for humans, plus the cost of a perpetual viewing chapel.

The world's only known commercial mummification facility is located in Salt Lake City, Utah. There, at a cost of several thousand dollars, one may have a corpse soaked in oil, herbs, wine, and other "secret" ingredients, then swaddled in linen, latex, plaster, gypsum and cement. The company, called Summum Bonum, does not include in its costs an optional mummiform, a hand-crafted pharaoh or Art Deco-style casting complete with jewels in which to encase the mummified remains, along with personal valuables. Cost for such jewel-encrusted mummiforms can exceed a million dollars.

Summum Bonum manager Al Greco reports that, while over 130 people have signed up for the mummification procedure, thus far only a Doberman pinscher and a cat have actually been mummified. Greco himself hopes to be mummified and then encased in a mummiform with his favorite wrench. The cost will likely exceed that incurred by a Chicago woman, who, in 1962, was found to have the mummified remains of her mother encased between two mattresses. For the 15 years prior to the discovery, inquiries about her mother's whereabouts had been fended off with "Mummy's sleeping."[3]

So it is that we have progressed from the charnel houses and ossuaries of Medieval Europe, where bones and skulls were warehoused in anonymity, to cryonics and weather-sealed vaults assuring indeterminate preservation. Among such wide-ranging choices lies an incredibly divergent mindset toward death and what, if anything, shall follow. Perhaps we answer our own questions about death simply in deciding what should be done with our remains when we die. Does it matter at all, only slightly, or in quite a profound way? There doubtless is no right or wrong answer, there is only personal resolution and conviction to rely upon as we seek to decide.

It takes a certain courage and maturity to openly confront such choices, but doing so may profoundly alter our interpretations of both life and death by forcing us to focus on that certainty that awaits each one of us. That certainly would seem to represent whatever reason we need to cherish what is ours until we die

Chapter Nine

Lessons In Stone—Can Cemeteries Impart Insight And Perspective?

The love of all men as equally mortal.
—Erik Erickson

How we choose to tend the dead represents a revealing aspect of our own relationship to personal death. Nowhere is there more tangible evidence of that interplay than in cemeteries. They reflect a timeless and seemingly universal human longing to revisit the dead, to tend the remnants of what we may wish we had tended to more earnestly in life.

Several years ago, my husband and I, while visiting in Hungary, walked, as we often do in our travels, through a cemetery. It was a Sunday afternoon and neither of us was prepared for what we were about to witness. Well into the cemetery, a crowd of several hundred people had gathered. Despite their numbers, they stood quietly, each one patiently awaiting his or her turn, each with a flower in hand.

Before them lay a mound of floral tributes some six feet high and as many feet wide. We looked on as they approached it, one by one, each placing his or her offering on the growing mass, each silently expressing condolences, and then stepping aside so that the person behind could do likewise. Among the group was a blind woman clasping a single white calla lily. When it was her turn, she was gently guided forward. You could see tears streaming down her face. "Who is being honored here?" I asked the man standing alongside me. "Nagy," he whispered, "Nagy."

Later we learned that Imre Nagy was an the prime minister of Hungary when he challenged the Soviet government country and led an uprising in 1956. His valor and conviction later cost him his life. Following his execution in 1958, his body was thrown over the wall of a prison where he had been held, later to be buried unceremoniously.

It is difficult to imagine a more evocative scene than the one played out at the gravesite of the martyred Imre Nagy. That which could no longer be shared with the living was being tenderly expressed to the dead. All such acts of kindness, across the reaches of time, were once again present there. So, too, were the ageless emotional lessons taught by the dead to the living—lessons in courage, sacrifice, generosity of spirit, gratitude, and what it means to care for the human condition.

The ancient Greeks referred to cemeteries as paideia, meaning a school. They believed that time spent there provided a source of understanding and perspective, that rather than negating life, contemplation would deepen its meaning. Even children were encouraged to participate in visits to the dead. Such visits, it was felt, helped to clarify the natural cycle of birth and death, and in doing so made the process more acceptable.[1]

In order to establish the proper environment for their places of learning, the Greeks carefully chose just where their cemeteries were to be located. As further testament to their love of beauty and the belief that it feeds the heart and inspires the soul, Greek cemeteries were graced with rich emblems of funerary art.

The Greeks exhausted the resources of their exquisite art in adorning the habitations of the dead. They discouraged interments within the limits of their cities; and consigned their reliques to shady groves, in the neighborhood of murmuring streams and merry fountains, close by the favorite resorts of those who were engaged in the study of philosophy and nature, and called them, with the elegant expressiveness of their own beautiful language, cemeteries, or "places of repose."[2]

In this country during the Romantic movement of the 19th century, a love of nature coupled with a desire to protect it against an ever-encroaching urban tide, fostered the creation of cemeteries not unlike those of the ancient Greeks. Both Green Wood Cemetery in Brooklyn, New York, and Mount Auburn in Cambridge, Massachusetts, attest to the revival of interest in cemeteries as a place of repose and contemplation. Such heavily wooded, idyllic environs appealed not only to the bereaved but to strollers and picnickers as well. Modeled on the Père Lachaise Cemetery in Paris, the sylvan mood was set by benches positioned along winding pathways, running water from brooks or streams, and tranquil ponds, all amidst stately ancient trees.

As with the Greeks, settings for such 19th-century cemeteries were further enhanced by elaborately carved gravestones and statuaries. Most were made of granite, which was less impervious to the elements than the marble employed in 18th-century gravestone carving. One might stroll past a weeping angel writing a passage in the

Book of Life with a feather quill, or crowns of laurel (symbolic of victory among the Greeks) atop shrouded urns.

During the first half of the 20th century, the elaborate and evocative grave markers so beloved by the Victorians gave way to more cookie-cutter-looking stones. Most were either rectangular or cylindrical (referred to as "pillows"). Gone, too, were the ornate iron fences designating a family plot. Gone were the benches that once looked like they had been pulled up to the grave for a visit. Cemeteries took on a more uniform look with straight pathways and fewer trees.

More and more, memorial parks replaced traditional cemeteries. Designed to appear as un-cemetery-like as possible, memorial parks usually required markers of one type only, which must be flush to the ground. The word cemetery was eliminated in favor of the less image-ridden word, "park". Maintenance was diminished, efficiency improved and the atmosphere substantially altered.

More and more often, death and everything attendant to it is disavowed and assiduously avoided. Only when absolutely necessary does one even go to a cemetery or a memorial park. Newly established burial sites, lying well outside the communities they serve, can be passed as one races along a freeway, without ever being noticed.

The Roman Empire, known for its fine system of roads and highways, placed cemeteries alongside each so that the dead would be regularly thought of by passersby. Roman gravestones were inscribed with such phrases as, "Today for me, tomorrow for you."

Some of our earliest cemeteries were located not alongside roadways but rather alongside the church. That practice, begun in Europe after the fall of the Roman Empire, reflected the belief that nearness to the church could protect the departed. Each Sabbath, those entering and leaving the church would walk among Puritan tablets embellished with such visuals as a skull and crossbones or a finger pointing toward heaven. Ever-present were reminders to mortals of the omnipotence of God and the frailty of human flesh, expressed in such epitaphs as: "Memento Mori"—Remember You Must Die, or "To Esse Mortatem"—You Are Mortal. Even inside the church the odor of rotting flesh, but yards away, might permeate the sanctuary.

Concerns over sanitation and pollution of water supplies from decaying corpses (sometimes embalmed with arsenic), church foundations weakened by ongoing excavation of graves, and a diminishing amount of church-yard space combined to end the use of churchyards as cemeteries.

Those designated to select alternate sites clearly did so with the Greek concept of beauty and repose in mind. A walk through almost any older cemetery—public or private, large or small—reflects that fact. Often, the burial ground selected is the high spot of the area, which, while not the most easily accessible, has the loveliest view.

The oldest existing cemetery in my own community is just such a place, sitting on a promontory that overlooks the river and park land below. It was first chosen as a burial site by Native Americans who inhabited the area almost 2,000 years ago. They fashioned mounds of earth, several feet in height, as grave markers for their dead. Beneath the mounds they dug out spaces for placement of skeletal remains, positioned facing east, toward the rising sun.

These Native American burial mounds now lie interspersed among gravesites of later area residents who likewise recognized the inspirational qualities of the setting and likewise adopted it as a cemetery site. At the time this occurred, in the early 1850's, some objected to the choice, feeling it inappropriate for Christians to be buried next to what they deemed heathens. Serious discussion arose over whether or not to remove the mounds, something that did not happen thanks to the wise counsel of the cemetery president. It was he who convinced his skeptical counterparts that all human burials are equally sanctified.

Unfortunately, attitudes like those of the objectors, which in retrospect may seem arcane, have not been exclusive to any time period or isolated to any one group of people. Racially segregated cemeteries, separation of Catholic from Protestant caskets by brick dividing walls at the time of burial (even those of married couples), and the denial of religious burials for suicide victims are but a few examples of how those entrusted to care for the dead have felt it appropriate to follow cultural biases.

And yet the grief felt by those Woodland Mound Builders so many centuries ago—was it any less personal than our own? And what of the countless others who followed them to weep alongside the graves of soldiers killed in the Civil War, infants and children who died from the influenza outbreak of 1917, wives lost in childbirth, parents and siblings who, one after another, died only weeks or months apart? How many tears were shed, how many hearts irretrievably broken? What stories are there, and if we knew each one, would the impact of knowing profoundly alter our own relationships and behaviors?

When you see how such tragedies were tenderly treated through representations such as an empty doll-sized rocking chair inscribed to "Our Darling Willie," or the stone likeness of a young maiden scattering flower petals over the site where the girl she was carved to represent lies buried, or the hands of granite clasped in memoriam to a devoted husband and wife symbolically inseparable, even in death—you see as well the timelessness of death's influence, its profound impact on who we are and on what we think and feel and do.

One of our abiding fears regarding death is the fear that we will be forgotten when we die. Certainly that was the case for many who died in times of famine, plague, or war. Today on Hart Island in New York City, there are daily burials of the unloved and nameless that remind us of our fear.

Hart Island is a mass pauper's graveyard for the indigent of New York, many of them children, victims of beatings or starvation. The first burial was that of an orphan named Louisa Van Slyke who had died at the Charity Hospital. Between her death in 1869 and 1938, some 425,000 interments took place. Each week over 150 corpses as well as arms and legs amputated in city hospitals are shipped to the island where convicts bury them in graves stacked three deep.

Our desire to memorialize the dead and our personal terror of ending up in circumstances like those of Hart Island is undeniable. Even there, approximately 50 to 150 bodies per year are disinterred and reburied by family members who finally have been able to identify the body or have managed to save up the money for a private service. Each year we spend millions of dollars for recovery of body parts lost in wars, explosions, accidents and natural calamities. And mostly we reject the idea of common graves, such as those at Hart Island, marked by a solitary stone cross bearing the inscription "He calleth his children by name."

At Piskarovske Cemetery in St. Petersburg, Russia, where half a million victims of the World War II German invasion lie buried in mass graves, there is likewise but a single marker designating the spot where each of the several thousand who died during a particular year of the siege were interred. At the far end of the cemetery stands a statue depicting "Mother Russia." Below her are inscribed the words, "We forget nothing, we forget no one."

Our guide for Piskarovske, a young man in his early 20's began to cry as we stood overlooking the eternal flame and the simple stone markers reading, "1942" or "1943," stretching in rows toward "Mother Russia."

"Do you have family buried here?" I asked him. "My grandfather," he said. "How often do you come here?" "Almost every day I bring visitors," he replied. "Does coming here always affect you this way?" "Oh yes," he acknowledged, "because I know that if it were not for them, the people lying buried here, I would not be alive, and it makes me grateful. Some were as young as I am, some younger when they died. Knowing that makes me live better because I try to live for them too."

Chapter Ten

Grief—Is It To Be Understood?

Ah, surely nothing dies but something mourns.
— Lord Byron

I was at my mother's bedside the morning she died. Her last utterance was my name, spoken not as a question but as an affirmation of my presence. Following her death, I chose to stay with her body. Placing my head next to hers on the pillow, I felt the curve of her neck, still warm and sweetly unperfumed just as I had always remembered it. She often told me what a snuggly baby I had been and how I would angle my head into the curve of her neck as she held me. My desire to snuggle there did not diminish with age and when she would tease me about always wanting to hug her, I would remind her that the word hug means "to soothe."

It was soothing, that last intimate moment with her before they arrived with the folding cot and the maroon-colored velvet bag for removal of her body to the funeral home. Just before they took her, I removed her wristwatch.

Clutching it in my palm, I was struck with the irony of how time represents all to the living and nothing to the dead.

It is strange how objects become the focus of our initial grief. When my friend Karen was murdered I remember seeing, at her home, a stack of Weight Watcher's dinners in the freezer next to the ice I was getting for a soft drink. More than anything else, those frozen dinners triggered my emotion. While going through my mother's closet to choose what they would dress her in for the casket, I saw my mother's shoes. My mother loved shoes and she loved to dance.

I thought back to all the times as a child that I had dressed up in her high heels and party dresses. My favorite shoes had been a pair of red kidskin stilettos, a gift from my father to her one Christmas. When we played dress-up at my grandmother's, I would always select from her cedar closet a peach-colored satin gown with pale blue ribbons that my mother had worn to college dances. I would imagine her gliding across the floor to music played by her favorite, "T. Dorsey." Her dancing days were over now. There remained the shoes.

When grief therapists treat people suffering from abnormal grief reactions, one thing they often do is to ask the person to bring in an object that belonged to the deceased. Discussion of the object's link to the deceased may lead to an acceptance of the person's death and thereby further the process of dealing with denial.

Grief is really about memories and associations. It is that intense longing to go back, and, as the drummer Gene Krupa said, "do it all one more time." The worst part of grief is knowing that we cannot. Objects left behind remind us of that.

Grieving has been described as the hardest work we are ever called upon to do. One reason why it is so difficult is because it's such a personal process. Since each of us grieves differently, there are no formulas or timetables or "how-to's" to aid us in the journey through bereavement. As a result, when we are working through our grief we feel as alone as we ever will.

How dreaded that sense of isolation and aloneness that is a part of grief. It numbs and disorients in ways that we could never believe. Over time it may diminish, but once upon us it never finally lets go. Like black holes in the universe, grief pulls and consumes, leaving a void that cannot be filled.

Part of grief is accepting the fact that the person we cared for is never to be heard or seen again. A friend of ours, who talked several times each day by phone to his brother, told of dialing that telephone number over and over again after his brother died. "I kept forgetting," he said, "that my brother wasn't going to answer."

Such manifestations of denial may be both necessary and beneficial as we mentally adjust to the facts of death. Prolonged and exaggerated denial, however, may be a sign of a circumvented mourning process. It falls upon those providing emotional support for the grieving, when appropriate, to gently remind them of reality and to encourage them to gradually face the loss.

Denial for the grief-stricken is disbelief that the individual so loved and relied upon has been forever taken from them. Sudden death can disorient people so fully that they cannot accurately identify their dead loved one. Some medical examiners and coroners feel that family members are the least likely to make a positive identification simply because they are in a condition of denial.

It was reported that Jacqueline Kennedy crawled onto the back of the limousine in which her husband was shot, not for self-protection but rather to retrieve fragments of his skull, one of which she carried with her into the emergency room. Her own anguished and understandable denial over the violent horror of witnessing his death perhaps lured her to believe that she could somehow mend his mortal wound, a common reaction to death, when we seek to do something to protect or please the dead since the loss has not yet been grasped.

Even anticipatory grief—knowledge that death is imminent—doesn't always diminish denial. Weeks and months afterwards we may still hear the dead person's voice or footsteps, see him in a crowd, smell his cologne or tobacco or speak of him/her in the present tense, all as attempts at denying his non-existence. It is not uncommon to experience a visit from the deceased, which may or may not be distinguishable from a dream.

During a grief-loss seminar, every member including myself described dream-like visits from the dead while we were sleeping. Were they dreams? It was hard to know at the time, so vivid and real did they seem. Why did they occur? Most in the group agreed that the dead had come back to give them permission to move on, to temper their grief, to know that the dead no longer suffered. Such experiences may cause the bereaved to question their own sanity, a question raised over and over again during the grieving process. One of the women in our grief seminar said that she thought she had lost her mind when she purchased a sofa, at a cost of several thousand dollars, following her husband's death. "I hate that sofa," she told us, "but at the time I wasn't myself."

It may be tempting to move or to redecorate as a way of escaping the environmental reminders of one's sorrow. Getting involved in another relationship to assuage the inescapable loneliness is often a temptation. Using alcohol or other drugs to obliterate the anguish, or even just spending money on replacement experiences or things, may seem to lessen the feelings of emptiness but such acts may offer only temporary comfort and relief.

Part of the unfinished business of grief has to do with deciding what to keep and what to let go of with regard to the deceased, and just how you intend to continue life without them. When George Burns' beloved wife Gracie Allen died, he found himself unable to sleep. Finally, he moved to her bed. After that he could sleep again. Audrey Meadows reportedly said that walking into her dead husband's closet and smelling his clothes was what helped her. Another woman said that wearing her husband's bathrobe each morning was her first step in coming to terms with life minus his presence. When I returned to teaching following my mother's death, I could not remember my students' names for an entire semester. During that same time, I would stand at my closet each morning, unable to make a decision on what to wear or to get myself dressed. It became such a problem that I finally resorted to writing down what I would wear each day on an index card. When I told a psychologist friend, she said, "Oh, I'm so relieved. I had the same problem and thought I was crazy."

Grief may seem like a form of mental illness as it disrupts, disorients and destabilizes our relationship with everyone and everything familiar. Because of that, many grief therapists recommend not making any major life changes within the first year following a death. Such decisions may only add to the survivor's feeling of loss of control. What was altered or discarded in the need to escape the haunting specter of grief and loss may be longed for, but irretrievable in the future. It may or may not be true that "time heals all wounds." But time is required.

Anger is one of the most overlooked emotional responses to death. It may emanate from feelings that the one who died has abandoned you, feelings of anger toward a higher being for allowing the death to occur, anger at the deceased for having somehow contributed to their demise, or anger with life and with the world in general because there is no one specific person or thing to blame. Many people view anger, whether related to grief or not, as a negative affective response and consequently refuse to express it directly, often chastising themselves in the process. Yet increasingly, grief therapists are encouraging the bereaved to confront their emotions, anger included, honestly and directly.

At a grief seminar, a nationally known therapist told of a client who could not come to terms with the death of his father. When questioned, the young man revealed an abiding fear of his dead father's temper and fear that continued to cripple his emotional well-being even after his father's death. The therapist recommended that the fellow visit his father's grave and tell his father just how he felt. When the young man returned to his therapist, he described how he had angrily shouted and screamed at his father for all the times he had been hurt. In an act of ultimate vindication, he urinated on his father's grave. Only then, he said, was the barrier to that overwhelming fear finally removed. He was then free to properly complete the grieving process.

In contrast was the case of a woman who was described by the funeral director during one of our class visits there. While clearly devoted to her husband, she had planned his entire funeral without showing any emotion. At the service, she remained stoically detached. During follow-up conversations with the funeral director, she would speak lovingly of her husband but refused to comment on how she was coping with his death. Two months later, the funeral director was called to the woman's home where she had died of undetermined causes. She could be diagnosed with nothing other than what was listed on her death certificate, which was "a broken heart."

In some cases survivors may feel a special need to justify their existence as a sort of payback to the dead. This is called "death guilt." One wonders about such people as Vincent Van Gogh, named for a dead older brother, who saw the tombstone with the name he then bore each time he ventured from his childhood home. The Great Caruso was the last of 18 children and the only one to survive childhood. Sigmund Freud jealously wished for the death of his infant brother. After the child died, Freud said he fainted whenever he thought of his dead sibling.

One of the most poignant stories shared by a student of mine involved him overhearing his parents discussing such a death, that of an older brother. Both parents wished aloud that it had been one of the other children who had died instead. "Our dead son would have turned out better than his siblings," they agreed.

It is human nature to idealize the dead. After all, they can make no more mistakes. Holding them up to the living as icons, however, may be both irrational and unfair. Survivors may feel they are paying the price of death guilt, the guilt of survivorship, the guilt of "why am I alive when they are not?"

John Kennedy was thrust into the role of politician and presidential contender following the death of his older brother Joseph Jr. Recent revelations about Princess Diana include the fact that after the death of an infant brother, her parents tried for another child because they desperately wanted to carry on the Spencer name and title. That child was a girl named Diana. And what of Ross Perot, whose name reportedly was changed to Ross at the age of 12, following the death of an older brother named Ross?

One survivor of the 1958 Our Lady of Angels School fire in Chicago was Michele McBride. Ninety-two of her classmates and three nuns died in that fire. McBride described what it was like to be a survivor, being told that the dead were the lucky ones who were called to heaven to be angels, and that those who lived must be brave and accept it as an act of God. During her senior year of high school, McBride had an emotional breakdown. Her problem, she said, was the need to "vent my mourning. I was drowning in unshed tears." According to McBride, "Therapy is vocalizing your emotions until you learn to accept them without feeling guilty. . . . One day I realized that I wasn't crazy, that I was just suppressing my feelings and that I could live a full life not haunted by fear." McBride's struggle with death guilt is illustrated by an incident in which a mother of one of the victims shouted at her, "Why did you live and my son die?" McBride's response to the woman was, "If only you knew how many times I have asked myself that same question."

Survivors of war may likewise struggle with death guilt. The final scene of the movie *Saving Private Ryan* reflects that fact, as Ryan asks to be told that he has lived a good life and been a good man, in order to justify his having lived when so many others did not. During World War II, Sir William Stephenson, in charge of British Intelligence Operations in the United States, gave the following prayer to Eleanor Roosevelt, who thereafter carried it with her in her purse.

Dear Lord,

Lest I continue my competent ways, help me to remember Somewhere out there a man died for me today. As long as there be war, I then must ask and answer, Am I worth dying for?[1]

In addition to death guilt, another element of grief may be something called "death anxiety," the fear that we will die from the same causes as our parent or sibling did and at about the same age. Death anxiety may also be related to the prospect of life without the parent—that buffer, protector, role model—for our own lives and conduct. When a parent dies, our sense of security in knowing there is someone who loved us in such a unique way departs with him or her.

No matter how difficult, the loss of a parent is considered by some grief therapists to be less traumatic than the loss of a child. Children represent the future. When they die their parents understandably grieve for the promise of what might have been.

Siblings may also find a child's death difficult. Oftentimes, problems associated with this difficulty may not manifest themselves until the child has become an adult. Statistically, over two-thirds of all marriages where a child has died end in divorce. Differences in the way people grieve, how they try to place blame for the death, and guilt and anger undoubtedly all contribute.

If the death of a child is by suicide, the problems of grief are much more complex. Any suicide raises the question in a survivor of whether the relationship or the love was insufficient. Survivors of suicide may try to deny the suicide out of feelings of shame or inadequacy.

It was psychologist Eric Fromm's belief that being alone is the most prevalent and pervasive fear of the living, and that much of our behavior is predicated on trying to escape that fear. Yet, alone is how we may feel as we undertake the task of mourning. Those around us may be able to offer the most comfort and support by allowing us to respond to three simple statements. One is to say, "Tell me about it," and then to listen without the "I know exactly how you feel" (probably no one really does) and without saying "When I lost. . . ." Another is to ask, "What can I do for you?" and doing it. A third is to say, "Let's talk about [the deceased]. Do you remember when . . . ?" Talking about the deceased is a means of affirming their being.

It may also be helpful to remember that what the grieving person probably does not need is unsolicited advice or any kind of unsought justification for the loss that has been endured. Suggesting that the deceased is "in a better place now," or "was needed by God," may not be what an individual suddenly alone and bereft may find comforting.

Each of us, men and women alike, are afraid of the intense emotional encounters related to death. What do we say or do if the grief-stricken person breaks down? What if they, or we, lose control? Better perhaps to avoid, repress, pretend or deny, better to do anything but face that morass of grief. But what is the price we will pay? Is it worth that price to have ignored and denied death? Is that what we really should be doing?

Increasingly, grief psychologists and counselors wonder whether there might not have been something therapeutic to the grief practices of our early culture, their intimacy with death and dying and grief, as opposed to our denial and avoidance of it.

Think of *Gone with the Wind* when Rhett and Scarlett's child died. Black wreaths draped the doors of their home through which mourners dressed in black crepe passed, leaving their black-bordered condolence cards. The child's corpse was kept at home, watched over by her grief-stricken father, who for days refused to allow her burial. Was it better that such a time of bereavement was clearly provided and followed? Could the grief itself be better handled on a more personal and prolonged basis? Did prescribed rituals of mourning, linking the living to the dead, help to release the anguish? Or, is it more realistic to allow someone the standard "three days off" for the death of a loved one, followed by the customary current assumption that the grieving person should be "back to normal" within a few weeks?

The multitudinous deaths that occurred during World War I are often blamed for changes in our grief customs. The changes more likely had to do with the increased mobility and secularism of the 20th century. The close-knit community response to death of the preceding century no longer existed—where people were born, lived out their lives and died. Showing one's utmost vulnerability at the time of death became less and less easy when one was surrounded more by acquaintances and strangers rather than by life-long friends. If a loved one died far away, the death might not even be known of or acknowledged. So removed from intimate details of one another's lives have we become that many among us have likely had the horrific experience of asking acquaintances where they've been or what has been happening in their lives, only to receive a response of "Well, my father died," or "My sister was killed,"—and then what?

Grief has always exacted from us the ultimate emotional toll. That fact was no different in the 1800's than it is today. But perhaps it is our way of living in the 20th century, our lack of time and tradition, of our inability to pardon or understand the bereaved, our seeming fear of the emotional forces intrinsic to death, or simply our hope to deny the realities of it at all—that leave us unhealed, without comfort, "crazy."

One day when we were discussing grief, one of my students asked how it was possible for me to talk with them about my mother's death. "Doesn't it make you sad all over again?" It was a foreign exchange student who answered the question far better than I could have by saying, "My mother is thousands of miles away. When I left her, I knew that we might never see one another again. For that reason, I had to make sure that everything was okay between us. Every morning and every night, be sure that things are okay between you and your parents. That way, if anything does happen, you can think of them in a good way and remember them without so much pain." Sage

Conclusion

Be Happy While You May

We bless Thee for our creation, preservation, and all
the blessings of this life . . .
                            —*The Book of Common Prayer*

Do you recall prayers from childhood that included blessings for those with whom you hoped to share another day? As a child did you fold your hands and perhaps kneel alongside your bed as you prayed? And then would someone tuck you in, kiss you goodnight, hold your hands or gently brush your cheek before leaving you to slumber? If you still say prayers, how do you end them now? For what or for whom do you pray?

What we pray for are blessings of being mortal. They are the blessings that enhance our being for as long as they remain ours, until we die. One might wonder how it can be said that, if all will be taken from us, there could be blessings in being mortal. Just what are those blessings, and how do we come to know them?

A few simple questions that we should be asking ourselves each day hold the answer: and they are these. What do I cherish most in life? What do I most love? And should it be taken from me, what would I most long for?

Life itself is the first and most obvious of our blessings—" . . . we bless Thee for our creation." Whatever our
personal beliefs regarding the source of human life, it is
ours. We are granted hours and days in which to fulfill
those purposes we deem worthy of our efforts and talents.
A lifetime of 70 years holds over 25,000 days for such
opportunity. The choices we make in determining how to
utilize this finite allocation extended to us are serious in
nature. We may choose to deny the certainty of death in
exchange for illusory peace. But we pay a price for such
complacency and deception. The time we allow to escape
us in wasteful pursuits can never be recaptured. Reality
will, at some point, force us to that realization. And it is
then that we suffer inconsolable regret and longing for
what is never again to be ours.

Such a consequence is avoidable if we instead
choose to acknowledge and accept, and then act upon our
mortal condition. Though clearly more difficult, the
rewards inherent to such a determination are incalculable.
A thorough consideration of our terminal state makes evident the value of each hour and day that we live. As we
carefully mete out the measure of our lives, what would
have seemed to be the curse of being mortal, its seeming
brevity, becomes one of its greatest blessings, and gratitude for our creation abounds.

More than all else, we may pray for the preservation
of relationships that guide and sustain us throughout our
lives. Perhaps no other blessings are more treasured than
those based on the company of others. The relationships
we know as a parent, a sibling, a soulmate, or a child,
become, over the course of their development, irreplaceable.

But death takes away that which we pray will
remain ours, leaving us to reckon with the permanent
impact of such a profound consequence. How do we sur-

render that which is irreplaceable, the dearest of our mortal blessings, to death? Most of us do so by seeking some form of assurance that the significance of our lives will transcend our death.

If there were an embodiment of such transcendence, for me it would be found in our hands. It is with our hands that we nurture and tend, comfort and caress, educate and encourage, convey fondness for one another and signal farewell. The hands that we held when we were little, that we offered in friendship or vowed in marriage, the hands that we closed in death all represent the same transcendent timelessness embodied in hands held forth to bless or forgive, acknowledging "the peace which passeth all understanding." The hands of the Buddha are folded in acceptance of the physical being's ongoing passage into nonbeing. The four hands of the Hindu god Shiva hold symbolic representations of death and rebirth within the individual as well as within the universe.

Physical loss due to the death of someone we love requires us to rethink and reconstitute our relationship to him or her. We may begin by searching our memory for every scrap and detail of what it was like to have had that person with us. We may allow ourselves to soften and highlight, recolor and erase. What was unique and endearing becomes ever more so through personal recollection, to which we may return again and again. And as part of that process we come to understand that our relationships with one another remain constant and do endure.

One hundred years from today each of us will at best be a photograph, perhaps a name on a grave marker somewhere or a notation in some obscure family history. A hundred years from today will mirror the 13 billion years that preceded our being, whatever it was like then, before we were born. But until then, we are alive, and we have been granted the mortal blessings of caring about and for each other. Nothing, not even death, can diminish the significance and meaning of that. The very significance and meaning for which we yearn continue both despite life's impermanence and because of it. The significance and meaning of each of our lives rests in the ways that we are remembered and the intensity with which we shall be missed.

Beyond there remain "all the blessings of this life." Could we ever hope to experience even a small portion of them—walking, reading, gardening, travel, sports, hobbies, pets, cooking, music, art, maybe even cleaning? We are offered an infinite range of possibilities and unlimited choices with which to occupy and amuse ourselves every minute, every hour, every day we are alive. And as if that were not enough, we have within each of us that most remarkable capacity to know and to understand.

Knowledge and understanding take us beyond the bounds of mortal limitations to the furthest reaches of our creative imaginings. They allow us to select from among all the artistic, literary, historical, mathematical, philosophical, religious and scientific endeavors of humanity. There we are free to explore and to wonder and to comprehend the rich legacy of our collective being.

A mature understanding of death CAN free us to live wisely and well. Once we fully realize the fact that we are going to die there emerges from such certainty a perspective which allows us to take nothing for granted. Time becomes precious, relationships paramount, and the daily pleasures of life delectable. Anticipating the certain loss of these temporal gifts compels us to embrace them. And as we do so we experience an abiding appreciation of, and gratitude for, blessings of being mortal.

Notes

CHAPTER ONE:

1. Goodman, Lisl M. *Death And The Creative Life.* New York: Springer Publishing Co., 1981, p. 163.

2. Ibid.

3. Rosenthal, Ted. *How Could I Not Be Among You?* New York: George Braziller, 1973.

4. Kilian, Michael. "Writing From New York." *Chicago Tribune,* August 2, 1989.

5. Lund, Doris. *Eric.* New York: Harper Collins, 1974, p. 318.

CHAPTER TWO:

1. Paz, Octavio. *New Perspectives Quarterly.* Winter, 1994.

2. Obituary of rapster Eric Wright, ("Eazy-E"). *Milwaukee Journal,* March 27, 1995, reprinted with permission of the Associated Press.

3. Lifton, Robert J. and Olson, Eric. *Living And Dying.* Orlando, Florida: Harcourt Brace, 1975, pgs. 76-87.

4. Becker, Ernest. *The Denial Of Death.* New York: The Free Press, 1973, p. 215.

5. May, Rollo. *Love And Will.* New York: W. W. Norton, 1969, p. 106.

6. Reeves, Thomas. *A Question Of Character—A Life Of J. F. Kennedy.* New York: The Free Press, 1991, p. 95.

7. *Living And Dying,* p. 76–87.

8. Ibid.

9. Becker, Ernest. *Human Character As A Vital Lie*, in Morgan, John C. and Richard L., *Psychology Of Death And Dying*. Sunnyvale, CA: Westinghouse Learning Press, 1977, p. 124.

CHAPTER THREE:

1. Tolstoy, Leo. *Anna Karenina*. Oxford: Oxford University Press, 1995 (Translated by Louise and Aylmer Maude), p. 348.

2. *The Quest To Die With Dignity—An Analysis Of Americans' Values, Opinions, And Attitudes Concerning End-Of-Life Care*. Appleton, WI.: American Health Decisions, 1997, p. 16–17.

CHAPTER FOUR:

1. "Love And Let Die." *Time Magazine*, March 19, 1990, p. 62.

2. American Bar Association Resolution On The Definition Of Death, 1975.

3. American Bar Association Resolution On The Definition Of Death, 1981.

4. "Euthanasia Wars." *The Economist.* June 21, 1997, p. 22.

5. Angell, Marcia, M. D. "Euthanasia In The Netherlands—Good News Or Bad?" *The New England Journal Of Medicine.* Vol. 335, #22, p. 1676.

6. Quoted from Orloff-Kaplan, Karen. Executive Director, Choice In Dying, Washington, D.C.

7. "Mourners Bid Farewell To Cruzan." *Las Vegas Journal/Sun.* December 29, 1990 (Reprinted with Permission of the Associated Press).

8.

CHAPTER FIVE:
1. Tillich, Paul. *The Courage To Be*. New Haven, CT: Yale University Press, 1952, p. 13–14.

2. *The Denial Of Death* p. 26.

3. "While Rumors Fly, An Autopsy Is Performed." *American Heritage*. May, 1995, p. 26–27.

4. O'Connor, Matt. "Homicide Rate Keeps Examiner Busy." *Chicago Tribune*, May 12, 1991.

5. Ibid.

CHAPTER SIX:
1. Grinsell, Leslie. *Barrow, Pyramid, And Tomb*. New York: Thames and Hudson, Inc., 1975, p. 133–143.

2. El Mahdy, Christine. *Mummies—Myth And Magic In Ancient Egypt*. London and New York: Thames Hudson, 1989, p. 57–68.

3. Kolatch, Alfred J. *The Jewish Book Of Why*. Flushing, NY: Jonathan David Publishers, 1981, p. 53.

4. Arriaza, Bernardo. "Chile's Chinchorro Mummies." *National Geographic*. March, 1995, p. 78.

CHAPTER SEVEN:
1. Camille, Michael. *Master Of Death*. New Haven and London: Yale University Press, 1996, p. 176.

2. Owen, Trefor M. *Customs And Traditions Of Wales*. Cardiff: University of Wales Press, p. 104–105.

CHAPTER EIGHT:

1.   Ettinger, Robert. *The Prospect Of Immortality.* 1964 (By permission of the Cryonics Institute).

2.   Ibid.

3.   "What Are We Going To Do With Mom and Dad?" *Spy Magazine,* May 1989, p. 79.

CHAPTER NINE:
1.   Everett, Letter of November 28, 1863, Massachusetts Historical Society.

2.   Story, Joseph "An Address Delivered On The Dedication OfTthe Cemetery At Mount Auburn," Joseph T. Edwin Buckingham, 1831, p. 9. For the Attic Kerameikos as a model for the rural-cemetery movement, see Blanche Linden-Ward, *Silent City On A Hill:* Landscapes Of Memory And Boston's Mount Auburn Cemetery,(Ohio State University Press, 1989, p. 92, 129–130, 192–193.

CHAPTER TEN:
1.   Stevenson, William. *A Man Called Intrepid.* Orlando, Florida: Harcourt Inc., 1976, p. 118.

Resources

Administration On Aging
927 15th Street NW 6th Floor
Washington, D.C. 20005
(800)-677-1116
www.aoa.dhhs.gov

All About Hospice: A Consumer's Guide
(202)-546-4759
www.hospice-america.org

American Counseling Association
5999 Stevenson Avenue
Alexandria, VA 22304-3300
(800)-347-6647
www.counseling.org

American Hospice Foundation
2120 L. Street NW Suite 200
Washington, D.C. 20037
(202)-223-0204

Association For Death Education And Counseling
638 Prospect Avenue
Hartford, CT 06105-4203
(800)-586-7503

Bereavement Services
Gundersen Lutherian Medical Center
1910 South Avenue
LaCrosse, WI 54601
(608) 791-4747 or 800-362-9567, ext. 4747
www.gundluth.org/bereave

Caregivers Survival Resources
P.O. Box 27790
Golden Valley, MN 55427
(763)-553-9783
www.caregiver911.com

Centering Corporation
P.O. Box 4600
1531 N. Saddle Creek Road
Omaha, NE 68104
(402)-553-1200
www.centering.org

Center To Improve Care Of The Dying
George Washington University Medical Center
2150 Pennsylvania Avenue NW
Washington, D.C. 20037
www.gwumc.edu/redir.htm

Foundation Of Thanatology
630 W. 168th Street
New York, NY 10032-3702
(212)-928-2066

Hospice Foundation Of America
2001 S. Street NW Suite 300
Washington, D.C. 20009
(800)-854-3402
www.hospicefoundation.org

International Institute For The Study Of Death
P.O. Box 63-0026
Miami, FL 33163-0026
(305)-936-1408

Midwest Bioethics Center
1025 Jefferson Street
Kansas City, MO 64105-1329
(816)-221-1100
www.midbio.org

Mourning Discoveries
Bereavement Support Services
114 Garrett's Grove
Whitesboro, NY 13492
800-589-3742 or (315) 736-6643
www.mourningdiscoveries.com
e-mail mdisppt@borg.com

National Family Caregivers Association
10400 Connecticut Avenue Suite 500
Kensington, MD 20895
(800)-896-3650
www.nfcares.org

National Hospice And Palliative Care Organization
1700 Diagonal Road Suite 300
Alexandria, VA 22314
(800)-658-8898
www.nhpco.org

Partnership For Caring: America's Voice For The Dying,
(formerly Choices In Dying)
1035 30th Street NW
Washington, D.C. 20007
(800)-989-9455
www.partnershipforcaring.org

Supportive Care Of The Dying
c/o Providence Health System
4805 NE Gilsan Rm 2E07
Portland, OR 97213

The Grief Recovery Institute
P.O. Box 6061-382
Sherman Oaks, CA 91413
(818)-907-9600
www.grief-recovery.com

The Well Spouses Foundation
30 East 40th Street PH
New York, NY 10016
(800)-838-0879
www.wellspouse.org

Bibliography

Agee, James. *A Death In The Family.* New York: McDowell-Oblensky, 1957.

Ariés, Philippe. *Western Attitudes Toward Death—From The Middle Ages To The Present.* Baltimore and London: The John Hopkins University Press, 1974.

Aronson, Jason and Simcha, Paul Raphael. *Jewish Views Of The Afterlife.* Northvale, NJ: INC, 1994.

Becker, Ernest. *The Denial Of Death.* New York: The Free Press, 1973.

Budge, Ernest A. Wallis. *The Egyptian Book Of The Dead (The Papyrus of Ani).* New York: Dover Publishing Inc., 1967, unabridged edition.

Budge, Ernest A. Wallis. *The Mummy*—Funeral Rites and Customs In Ancient Egypt. London: Senate, 1975.

Camille, Michael. *Master Of Death—The Lifeless Art Of Pierre Remeit, Illuminator.* New Haven and London: Yale University Press, 1996.

Camus, Albert. *The Myth Of Sisyphus And Other Essays.* New York: Knopf, 1955.

Choron, Jacques. *Death And Western Thought.* New York: Macmillan Publishing Co., Inc., 1963.

Friedman, Russell and James, John. *The Grief Recovery Handbook—The Action Program For Moving Beyond Death, Divorce and Other Losses.* New York: Harper Perennial, 1998.

Garland, Robert. *The Greek Way Of Death.* Ithaca, NY: Cornell University Press, 1985.

Goodman, Lisl M. *Death And The Creative Life*. New York: Springer Publishing Company, 1981.

Grof, Stanislav and Christina. *Beyond Death—The Gates of Consciousness*. London: Thames and Hudson, Ltd., 1980.

Grollman, Earl A. *Concerning Death—A Practical Guide For The Living*. Boston: Beacon Press, 1974.

Grollman, Earl A., ed. *Explaining Death To Children*. Boston: Beacon Press, 1967.

Gunther, John. *Death Be Not Proud*. New York: Random House, 1953.

Hadas, Moses. *The Stoic Philosophy Of Seneca—Essays And Letters Of Seneca*. New York/London: W.W. Norton and Company, 1958.

Harrold, Joan and Lynn, Joanne. *Handbook For Mortals—Guidance For People Facing Serious Illness*. New York: Oxford University Press, 1991.

Kramer, Kenneth. *The Sacred Art Of Dying—How World Religions Understand Death*. New York/Mahwah: Paulist Press, 1988.

Kübler-Ross, Elisabeth. *On Death And Dying—What The Dying Have To Teach Doctors, Nurses, Clergy, and Their Own Families*. New York: Macmillan Publishing Co., Inc., 1969.

Levine, Stephen. *Healing Into Life And Death*. New York: Doubleday (Anchor Books), 1987.

Lifton, Robert J. and Olson, Eric. *Living And Dying*. Orlando: Harcourt Brace, 1975.

Mitford, Jessica. *The American Way Of Death Revisited*. New York: Knopf, 1998.

Neuland, Sherwin B. *How We Die—Reflections On Life's Final Chapter.* New York: Knopf, 1994.

Noll, Peter. *In The Face Of Death.* New York: Viking, 1989.

Penny, Nicholas. *Mourning.* London: Her Majesty's Stationery Office For The Victoria And Albert Museum, 1981.

Rinpoche, Sogyal. *The Tibetan Book Of Living And Dying.* San Francisco: HarperCollins, 1992.

Ruitenbeek, Hendrik M. *Death Interpretations.* New York: Dell Publishing Co., 1969.

Singh, Kathleen Dowling. *The Grace In Dying.* San Francisco: HarperCollins San Francisco, 1998.

Sonsino, Rabbi Rifat and Syme, Rabbi Daniel B. *Jewish Views Of Life After Death.* New York: UAHC Press, 1990.

Staniforth, Maxwell. *Marcus Aurelius—Meditations.* London: Penguin Books, 1964.

Sullivan, Lawrence E. *Death, Afterlife, And The Soul.* New York/London: Macmillan Publishing Company/Collier, 1987.

Tolstoy, Leo. *The Death Of Ivan Ilych.* London: Oxford University Press, 1960.

Toynbee, Arnold. *Man's Concern With Death.* New York: McGraw-Hill, 1968.

Vernant, Jean-Pierre. Mortals And Immortals—Collected Essays. Princeton: Princeton University Press, 1991.

Webb, Marilyn. *The Good Death—The New American Search To Reshape The End Of Life.* Westport, CT: Greenwood Press, 1997.

Wiesel, Elie. *Night.* New York: Bantam Books, 1982.

Willis, Gary. *Lincoln At Gettysburg—The Words That Remade America.* New York: Simon and Schuster, 1992.

Index

Other outstanding books from North Star Publications

The Shadow Side of Intimate Relationships
What's Going on Behind the Scene
Douglas & Naomi Moseley

"Doug and Naomi Moseley are experts when it comes to the underbelly (shadow side) of relationships. This book is a must read for folks who desire a deeper understanding of marriage dynamics."

John Bradshaw

"A real book for real people who are lost in power struggle and want to find their way to love and passion in marriage."

John Gray, Ph.D. Author, *Men Are from Mars, Women Are from Venus*

"With incredible clarity, uncompromising truth, and rare and refreshing wisdom, the Moseleys have written a life-changing book that will help couples create profoundly intimate relationships.!

Marriage magazine

Your Guy's Guide to Gynecology
Everything You Wish He Knew About Your Body
If He Wasn't Afraid To Ask
Bruce Bekkar, MD & Udo Wahn, MD

"Dr. Bruce is loving, wise, insightful, brilliant, and as funny as Dave Barry. You'll love this book!"

Mark Victor Hansen, Co-author, *Chicken Soup for the Soul® series*

"Not just for guys-this is a must-read for couples. A great opportunity to have open discussion between the sexes. This should help demystify the gynecologist's office for the partners of our patients.

Raquel D. Arias, M.D. Associate Dean for Women & Associate Professor of Obstetrics and Gynecology U.S.C. School of Medicine

". . .smart, funny and informative. It should be required reading for any man who cares about women."

Marilu Henner
Actress and New York Times best-selling
Author, *Marilu Henner's Total Makeover*

Coming from North Star, February 2002

Wrestling with an Angel
Dreams and Stories of Men in Change
Jerre J, Sears, Ph.D.

Few men can discuss what is happening to them when going through profound changes. Many even do not understand that they are changing, but the unconscious knows and reveals it in explicit dreams.

Author and expert Jerre Sears, Ph.D., reveals the dreams and true stories of men undergoing profound change. He interprets the dreams and the effects they have had on the individuals. He also reveals how the internal changes affected the lives of the dreamers.

Women who read this book will understand the changes men experience and the problems they have in dealing with change. Men will find a reference point to work from which allows them to see that they are not alone in their worlds of change.

The author/therapist specializes in men's issues. He knows whereof he speaks, for he himself went through a major change after a powerful transforming dream.

As a result, he changed his career, his lifestyle and, most importantly, the way he relates to people.

Dr. Sears gives us a clear and easily readable book to ponder as well as a tool to understand the process of change in men.

About The Author

Margo Drummond has spent the past 25 years teaching and learning about the meaning and consequences of human death.

Over 2,000 students have taken a course she developed and taught called, Death And Dying-Issues Of Living And Life.

She has traveled the world gathering information on the death customs and beliefs of other cultures. Insights from professionals who deal with death on a daily basis as well as lengthy service as a cemetery commissioner have further enriched her understanding of this timeless topic.